More Prince Edward Island Tales

**Poems and Stories
by members of the
Montague Library Writers Guild**

More Prince Edward Island Tales

Copyright 2010. by the respective writers and photographers. All rights reserved. No part of this book may be used in any form or by any means "graphical, electronic, or mechanical" without written permission of the copyright owners. Purchase and author-contact information is available from the publisher:

    Wood Island Prints
    670 Trans-Canada Highway, RR 1
    Belle River, PE C0A 1B0
    (902) 962-3335 schultz@pei.sympatico.ca

For information about the Writers Guild you may contact:
    Swarna Chandrasekera, Librarian
    Montague Public Library
    Montague, PE C0A 1R0
    (902) 838-2928 montague.gov.pe.ca

Printing and binding by:
    Lightning Source Inc. (US)
    1246 Heil Quaker Blvd.
    La Vergne, TN 37086 USA
    Voice: (615 213-5815
    Fax: (615) 213-4725
    Email: inquiry@lightningsource.com
    www.lightningsource.com

    Production of this book was subsidized by a grant from the Southern King's Arts Council

ISBN 986-0-9866065-0-2

Introduction

The members of the Montague Library Writers Guild are pleased to present another collection of their stories and poems for your enjoyment.

All contributors are members of the Guild and, at the present time, we meet the third Wednesday of every month at the Montague library located in the Cavendish Farms Montague Wellness Centre. The address of the Wellness Centre is 53 Wood Islands Rd., Montague, PE., C0A 1R0

At the meetings we share, discuss and critique our writings with the goal of encouraging each other and sharpening the quality of our work. It has been through the inspiration of the various members that these books have come to fruition. Visitors, guest speakers and new members are always welcome at our meetings. There are no fees to become a member.

The Guild has expanded its activities to include public readings and sharing of the writing process. As a group, or individually, we have entertained audiences at Perrin's Villa, Montague Summerfest, Wood Islands Ferry Festival, The Arts Center, Ceilidhs, and various schools in the region.

We would like to thank our editor/publisher, Tom Schultz, for his time and dedication in getting this book to print. Also a special thanks to any of our partners, husbands or wives, who have helped review our work and to Montague Librarian, Swarna Chandrasekera, for all her support and encouragement.

We hope you will enjoy reading our latest book as much as we had the pleasure of writing about our beautiful Island.

Joanne Collicott McGuigan, President
Montague Library Writers Guild

More Prince Edward Island Tales

Loman Bell..*1*
   Canada Our Great Nation.........................*3*
   Hopefield Farmer......................................*4*
   Coming Home...*6*
   Seeds You Sow...*7*
   We've Loved Life......................................*9*
   The Wind Blows......................................*10*
   How Far is Heaven?................................*11*
   The Fury Does Blast...............................*12*
   Working At the Park...............................*13*
   Berry Picker's Lament............................*14*
   Homeland..*15*

Joanne Collicott McGuigan........................*17*
   Between Red Rocks and Wild Roses.........*19*
   Blue Moons and Other Moons.................*21*
   Will You Hear the Banshee Cry?.............*25*

Tom Rath..*31*
   Bargain!..*32*
   Island Foods—It Doesn't Get Any Better Than This.*34*
   Harness Racing.......................................*35*
   Lighthouses—Beckoning Beacons...........*37*
   PEI Maple Syrup....................................*40*
   The Best Souvenir..................................*42*
   Shoreline Harvest..................................*43*

Tom Schultz...*45*
   Driving in the Dark................................*46*
   Incredible Supplemental Health Care.......*48*
   Wood Heat...*51*
   Sailing to Victoria..................................*53*

Kim Smith..*63*
   Prince Edward Island is Not Vancouver Island....*64*
   Things I Never Said Before Moving to PEI.........*69*
   Moving Coast to Coast to Live Our Dream.........*71*

An Island Evening	75
Coyotes	76
The Farm Wife's Lament	78
My Life in P.E.I. an Update	82

Linda Stewart ... 83
Cow's Milk	84
Simple Country Pleasures	85
Rich in Simplicity	85
My First Visit to Woolworth's	86
Looking for Partridge	86
Sweet Offerings	87
Marjorie's Place	88
My Island	90
Kitchen Sounds	91
Native Islander	92
Ordinary Things on Ordinary Days	93
Coffee	94
Morning Walk	95
October on the Island	96
Winter Landscape	97
A Boy and His Chickens	98
Almost Ten	99
Profile of an Eleven Year Old	100
Love Notes in the Sand	101

Leslie Stewart ... 103
Bizarre	104
Grandchildren Come To Stay	106
Panmure Island	108
Memories of Mine	109
Vanessa	110
Day Dreaming	112
Look What the Storm Brought In	114
Voices We Hear	116
Sands of Time	118

Loman Bell

Loman Bell was born on Prince Edward Island, in southern King's county. He was raised in a little village called Murray River—a close, family-oriented community—in the nineteen fifty's with lots of family and friends. Murray River School began his education. His father was a fisherman, farmer, mechanic, and general jack of all trades while his mother was a fish plant worker and general labourer, as well as a Godly mother and housewife. Both were active in music: singing and playing at church as well as other community functions. They lived and worked in the Village until job opportunities drew them to Charlottetown and later Quebec.

Loman started at an early age singing for fun for family and friends. This love of music took him on many different journeys, across Canada and the US singing, writing, and playing instruments. As he says, "It always seemed a real adventure, from playing and singing in church from a very young age, even in the music festival in Montague around the mid fifty's, then on the road meeting the music scene across north America. Playing on the street corners in Vancouver for spare change was a real bit of fun and chance to meet lots of people from around the globe, Also to conventions across the states in places like Pennsylvania, Prentice Main, And of course here on the Island at street meetings."

"This writing of poetry and short stories has been lot's of fun so far and I hope to continue doing it for lot's of years yet. I have a new book coming out called *Facing The Future* which has lots of real interesting material about the times we're living in plus making plans about the future."

He is the author of *House of Angels*, a book about his life and experiences with God. Email him at *lombell@yahoo.ca* or check out his material on you tube, I tunes, *www.amazon.com* or his web home page at *www.angelsalive.net*

Loman Bell: Canada Our Great Nation

Canada Our Great Nation

*The Fathers of Confederation,
Planned this to be a great nation.
For all the people, they found a solution,
We must agree on a constitution.*

*Canada is one great country,
We all love to keep it free.
Everyone has this resolution,
We must agree on the constitution.*

*Prime minister is coming, the city is humming,
With news that the premiers will meet.
Keep Canada together, even through this stormy weather,
Respect the rights of all people the same.*

*In 1864 the wheels began turning,
With pen in hand, the midnight oil was burning.
Put our heads together, part of creation,
Unite our country in confederation.*

*Have a referendum from the east coast to the west,
We all love our country and want it to be best.
Talk to each other, let peace dominate,
Now, light the darkness, before it's too late.*

*The cradle of confederation, rocks once again,
To still the tempest in our souls, soothe the hearts of men.
Let wisdom speak to our minds, and truth lead us on,
There are brighter days coming, if we will work along.*

Hopefield Farmer

*Up with the sun, working away,
Driving the mail, on his way.
Cows to milk, chores to be done,
All the way, 'till setting sun.*

*Just a Hopefield farmer, hoping for rain,
To water the ground, help grow the grain.
Then he'll plough the field, and start again,
Another year to plant, harvest and gain.*

Loman Bell: Hopefield Farmer

Trying to get by, bills to pay,
Not too much money, bailing hay.
Work in the woods, hard day's task,
Drive the mail, if my car will last.

Time goes by, everybody knows,
Sometimes it's fast; sometimes it's slow.
God made us all, to see Him one day,
Then he'll plough those fields, till judgment day.

Now time has come, finished with the mail,
Many years of service, through rain, snow, and hail.
Work is never finished, still the farm to run,
Pray for health and happiness, with each new day's sun.

Coming Home

I've worked on the west coast, working mighty hard,
From factory, to picking fruit, and the old train yard.
Fields to harvest on the prairies, growing lots of grain,
Still homesick for my roots, coming back home again.

Coming home again, I'm coming home again,
Where the sea gull's call, speaks my name.
Coming home again, coming home to stay,
The special little place, by the water's sway.

Worked through central Canada, with all the beauty there,
Cities stretch for miles—shipping everywhere.
Take me to the country, with lots of room to roam,
Coming back to my Island, treasure down home.

No matter where you live, from the east coast to the west,
This land so full of splendour—God's handiwork at it's best.
I live on a special Island, it's where I belong,
A little garden paradise, a hospitality's song.

Seeds You Sow

Yes! I know God loves country people,
He loves city people to.
Together down these same old highways,
Remembering God's golden rule.

I thank God for all those country roads,
Where I used to walk when but a lad.
Whatever seed you sow, that's the seeds you'll have to grow,
And reap the harvest someday.

Just to hear dad singing Lily Of The Valley,
How those songs rang across my mind.
Mother reading from the good old Bible,
About all those promises so divine.

God blessed this house to be a shelter for me,
A strong tower to live in day and night.
Storms of life beat upon the walls,
Still they withstood the winds all right.

My heart cries out! Thanks for all the memories,
Run like a river—all the footsteps back to you.
My longing desire for those peaceful country roads.
I need to never forget what I've been through.

More Prince Edward Island Tales

We've Loved Life

We've strolled together on the shore,
Hand in hand more and more,
Laid on the beach at sunset,
Satisfied together since we met.

Watch waves come in from the sea,
Crashed on the sand full and free,
Life we've lived here all our days,
And it's so grand in all its ways.

Another day to live so free,
Time passing by we all can see.
Cautiously step in each day at a time,
We always walk close to the line.

Each face has its own story,
Complete with the pain and glory.
Each person on earth still has needs,
Some He receives; some He heeds.

Does all mankind shed a tear,
If we don't have comfort living here,
We all need love everywhere,
And should want some love to spare.

For a brighter tomorrow we try to prepare,
This vast creation has room to spare.
We're part of the picture—every one must be—
If we wait for tomorrow, then we will all see.

The Wind Blows

*The wind blows, it's so revealing,
Of a power, not made by hands,
It is sometimes smooth and gentle,
Sometimes rebels, destroys the land.*

*Whatever reason, we're part of creation,
Presentation, of nature's plan.
Rich or poor, we're in it together,
Plan for the future, it's in our hands.*

*The grains and flowers, the grass and the land,
The wind in the sails, the sea on earth's span.
The wind moves, we see results so grand,
Like a gigantic structure, of a Master plan.*

*The wind is blowing, do you hear it speak?
A voice of command, not very weak,
This whole creation, made for man so meek,
Affects everything, even as we seek.*

Loman Bell: How Far is Heaven?

How Far is Heaven?

It happened one cold autumn; leaves began to fall,
We lost our Dad—He heard the Master call.
Another light is shining, on streets of glory land:
My dad; the angels took Him, in the Master's plan.

The leaves change colour, so beautiful to see,
Soon they end their season; the leaves are set free.
Like all things on earth, a season to grow and die,
We came as a baby; soon it's time to say goodbye.

Life's so brief, must be more than what we can see,
Money, fame, all those things, like living happily.
Feel the storm, hear Him warn, we'll soon be leaving here,
Could be our chariot's ready—home to our Saviour dear.

All life's journeys can be full of troubles and pain,
Stormy waters or high mountains, we travel through in loss or gain.
Let Jesus guide the way to travel, in the daytime or the night,
He shows the path, He knows the end of all, both wrong or right.

More Prince Edward Island Tales

The Fury Does Blast

*The wind does blow the trees to and fro,
The house gives a little creak and sigh.
By the windows, in the gale, the leaves do blow,
Hold secure 'till the storm passes by.*

*The wind does increase from a gale to a blast,
Swaying trees—will they hold to their roots?
You wonder, through this, will anything last,
Rain comes in fury—we grab our boots.*

*Hear a big crack; now lightning in the storm,
Thunder rumbles; feel the shake in the floor.
Are the lightning rods secure? Are they too worn?
Latch the windows and brace the door.*

*In the midst of the tumult, trees start to fall,
Pieces blowing—some roof shingles as well.
On this foundation, the house will stand tall,
Most important, through the night, we can tell.*

*The power starts to flicker, then it's gone,
Grab a candle, flashlight, oil lamp strong.
Batteries for the radio—will it last? How long?
Contact with others, in this storm going on.*

*Time passed by; the storm moves along,
Go outside; when the wind has gone.
Leaves, branches everywhere down the lane,
The storm passed by, never caused too much pain.*

Loman Bell: Working At the Park

Working At the Park

*Working at the park through light and dark,
Most times hard, to stay on the mark.
It will build muscle, if you stand the hustle,
Don't go astray, don't run away.*

*People come from near; some come from afar,
On a bike or motorhome, maybe a car.
There's camping, tenting, bonfires or swim,
The time you're there, regulations will win.*

*Parties start grooving, people start moving,
State the regulation, be kind and soothing.
Don't mean to ruin your fun, think of every one,
Some travel with the sun, in the good old summer fun.*

*Soon the fall winds blow; it's getting cold we know,
Kid's back to school, traffic slowing the flow.
Well the crew's doing good, hope to see you next time,
Working at the park, where we're all on the line.*

*Sometimes it's hard, to make things work,
You got a job, if your duties you don't shirk.
Working at the park, it'll give you pay,
Long, as the sun shines, sometime in the day.*

Berry Picker's Lament

Berry pickers picking berries,
Getting ready for the fall.
For jamming time with the pot a boiling,
When they're ripe you'll hear the call.

Come on sunshine dry the ground up,
We're dressed and ready to go.
Hit the trail to fill the bucket,
Get-em all before the snow.

Blast those pesky little ant hills,
Yes there's always one around.
Sometimes it seems the ground is crawling,
Grab them by the head if they're nice and round.

Will it rain or will the sunshine,
Dry the ground till my count is full.
They look so good the red and blue ones,
But the green ones we don't pull.

Making a batch of jam before sundown,
The big pot a boiling you gotta stir.
Got the jars but not enough berries,
Back to the patch earlier next year.

I'm so glad for these sweet little berries,
Yet the pain of the pickers I feel.
So this lament I'll sing at berry picking time,
And hope all the ones I picked are real.

Homeland

The stars shine brighter,
Over this little Island home.
The moon shines its light,
On this Island never alone.
We'll walk here in freedom,
With care for each one.
Thank God for creation,
A gold nugget we've won.

It's our home we love,
God keeps it safe and true.
Our children can run and play,
Enjoy the skies so blue.
Neighbours help each other,
When we need an extra hand.
Time passes—we enjoy life,
Loving our dear homeland.

Day by day we work and labour,
Toil and sweat, each woman and man.
Tells the tale of survival,
Our families had a plan.
In the mornings work in daylight,
Others toil in shifts as well.
Endure throughout the seasons,
Times change, the truth will tell.

Joanne Collicott McGuigan

Joanne Collicott McGuigan lives with her husband, Wayne, and their cat, Angel, a few kilometres south of Montague, P.E.I. Joanne considers herself, not *from away*, but an *Islander by marriage*. Her husband's ancestors, Jack "Jock" McGuigan and wife Peggy Hughes, emigrated from Co. Monaghan, Ireland and arrived in Prince Edward Island around 1840. They settled in the St. Mary's Road area.

Since meeting in Oshawa, Ontario, Joanne and Wayne spent every summer on the Island, and now they live here permanently. Joanne feels it is exactly like Lucy Maude Montgomery, author of *Anne of Green Gables*, said, "Once you come to the Island you feel you have come home."

The oldest of five children, Joanne spend her childhood in the province of New Brunswick. In the spring of 1997, New Brunswick was connected to P.E.I. by the Confederation Bridge. The bridge is a distance of 12.9 kilometres and the longest bridge over ice-covered waters.

Joanne enjoys walking in the fresh air and listening to Celtic music, such as played here in the Maritimes. The secrets of the mind, the universe and the betterment of mankind have always been important interests to her.

Joanne's parents met during the 2nd World War in England where her mother was a nurse. Her mother was from Co. Mayo, Ireland and her father a Canadian soldier from Canterbury, New Brunswick.

Although working in the banking field in Oshawa, Ontario,

was Joanne's primary profession, for a time she also wrote a dream analysis column for a local paper. Another article by Joanne is a story about her mother, Catherine Collicott, being a War Bride. It is available to read at Canada's Immigration Museum, Pier 21, Halifax, Nova Scotia.

Other books by the author available at amazon.com are: *Child of Danaan*, a story about the loss of Joanne's son and *The Dream Mechanism*, a compilation of the dream analysis column. She also contributed pieces to the first Writers Guild book.

Between Red Rocks and Wild Roses

Pockets almost empty,
Cupboards nearly bare.
He can't find enough stamps,
Looked for work everywhere.

With the last of the cash,
He booked a Charlottetown flight,
Then left the sweetheart behind
To face a long lonely night.

It's a touch down in Toronto,
Then onward further west,
Towards the draw of the oil sands,
Where the money is best.

He's working twelve hour days,
Braving the harsh winter cold,
Sweating nights in a camp
Dreaming of the old fishin' hole.

Amongst fellow Maritimers,
He is never quite alone.
Their tall tales of the sea
Make him lonesome for home.

Evenings by crackling fires,
Someone picks at the strings.
While others play poker,
A few of them start to sing.

Then it is home to see Mother.
He brought a new shinin'
   truck,
Filled with a bittersweet smell
Of Wild Rose Country good
   luck.

*He stays home for a few weeks
Then flies back to the West.
The brand new rig is left
For the sweetheart to test.*

*He emails her daily
With passionate needs,
"Please, pretty lady,
Come to the West with me."*

*Time marches by quickly
And he's surprised to retort,
"Three years have suddenly passed
And the nest egg's still short."*

*Like everyone else
Who sings the same song.
He never intended to stay
  away
From the Island so long.*

*Between red rocks and wild
  roses,
His head and heart never
  meet,
Wondering where back home
  befits
These cowboy boots on his
  feet.*

Blue Moons and Other Moons

Now many times have you heard the expression, "That will happen once in a Blue Moon?" It is not as farfetched as you may think. *Once in a Blue Moon* is an expression that has been around for a few hundred years. It simply means whatever is referred to will not happen often, whether it is winning the lottery, having your secret desires fulfilled, or some other unlikely scenario.

Just last week at a cribbage game I heard someone say, "It's been a Blue Moon since I've had a good hand!" That may be a bit of a playful exaggeration but it fully explains the disappointment in not getting good cards for quite some time.

The difference between a Blue Moon and any other full moon is that all 12 months have *one* full moon but roughly once every three years there is a month with *two* full moons. The second full moon of the month is a Blue Moon.

This past December (2009) there was the unusual occurrence in the sky with two full moons in the month—the first on December 2 and the second, known in folklore as a Blue Moon, on December 31, New Years Eve. Throughout this century, a Blue Moon will appear only three times on New Year's Eve. The next year-end Blue Moon will be in 2028.

From everything I have read or heard, the Blue Moon seems to be thought of as a *Lover* or *Maiden Moon*. It is the time when the Lady in the Moon smiles down on our beautiful planet and inspires the ladies to propose to the man of their choice. This is similar to the tradition associated with Leap Year Day (February 29), when the women can have the honour of popping the question to the men.

I found an old song where Hank Snow and Anita Carter sang, "When my Blue Moon turns to gold again, you'll be back within my arms to stay." Then there is the bluegrass singer, Bill Monroe, singing, "Blue Moon of Kentucky, keep on shining. Shine on the one that's gone and left me blue." These words seem to imply a Blue Moon is a Lover's Moon and bodes well for bringing star-crossed lovers back to each other.

Most full moons of the twelve months have names—*Harvest Moon, Hunter's Moon,* etc. Here on Prince Edward Island I have heard one called a *Mackerel Moon* by friends who were thinking of fishing mackerel. In that case, the gray clouds that passed in front of the moon were peppered with irregular spots of red. The mackerel were plentiful the next day—maybe that moon does hold the secret of the mackerel.

Another interesting full moon is the *Wishing Moon*. You don't have to be an Irish Druid to know the tradition of invoking the spirit of the Wishing Moon. Followers of the old religion would use the time of the Wishing Moon to make a list of their hopes and wishes for the future and then bury the list in some earth. Perhaps they would just stand outside, under the moon rays, proclaiming their inspirations and hoping they will come to fruition.

The Wishing Moon is the first full moon after the fire festival of each of the four seasons celebrated by the druids. These festivals were celebrated for three days, before, during and the day after this full moon. One of these festivals, know now as *Halloween*, has carried down through the years. Adults and children still celebrate it every year by dressing in disguise for costume parties, going trick or treating, and putting up decorations with imagery of death and the supernatural.

On the eve of Halloween coming into November 1, *Samhain*, meaning summer's end, was celebrated as a fire festival by the Druids. It is known as a time when the gateway to winter opens and the veil to the Otherworld was thin enough to peer into. This was also known as the night when the souls of the dead could leave their realm and wander through ours. Other fire festivals were held on February 2—called *Imbolc*—and another for the beginning of summer—called *Bethane*—held on May 1. Lastly, there is *Lughnasadh* which commemorates the beginning of the harvest. The Wishing Moon is the first full moon following each of these fire festivals.

Since being a small child I have heard stories on how the rays of any of the full moons can have an adverse affect on certain people making them more prone to emotional outburst. If the moon affects the ebb and flow of the tides of the ocean then it would stand to reason the moon could affect our physical body which is made up of a high percentage of water.

"By the way you are acting, I think the full moon got you tonight!" My mother could often be quoted as saying. She meant that the rays of the full moon had caused the person to act differently. Perhaps he or she had drunk too much, argued unreasonably, or perhaps become quite unruly around the time of the full moon that particular month. Mother would say, "Don't start something on the full moon that you want to finish quickly. The full moon may bode well for love but not for other issues."

If my dear departed Mother had to say that about the full moons, I would love to hear what her theories would be on the blue moons and the reactions its rays could draw out.

If we let our imagination run a little wild we can see figures in the full moon. I see the kind face of a woman who smiles benevolently down on us mere mortals. Others see different shapes in the moon, whether it be a man or an animal figure. Some people believe the dead go to the moon. I was told by one girl that she sees the faces of her deceased parents in the full moon. Scientists would say these images are caused by the hills and valleys of the moon, but that does not dispute the fact that these hills and valleys make up a face that is projected to us on this planet.

After the Blue Moon of December 31, 2009, there were a couple days of fine weather, then quite high winds and lots of snow on Prince Edward Island. All in all it was a mild January with the temperature staying just around the freezing point. Then the news was flooded with stories of the earthquake in Haiti—the worst earthquake in two centuries. It left a terrible devastation with thousands of people dead. This happened only 14 days after the year-end Blue Moon.

Whether a Full Moon or a Blue Moon, it may be a good time to take stock of your life. As for me, like the druids of olden times, I will try to celebrate the full moons and say an extra prayer for protection the three days, before, during and after these moons. Having a cozy fire in the stove or being outside with a crackling campfire burning might add some ambiance. Who knows, this may help curtail personal upsets and the natural disasters that have followed *Once In A Blue Moon*.

Will You Hear the Banshee Cry?

Maggie carefully set her coffee cup beside her laptop on the old maple desk. This had been her ritual nearly ever morning since the computer had first entered into the household five years earlier. As she glanced out the southeast window, the sun rays were starting to peek out from amongst the softwood trees surrounding the perimeters of the lawn. Even the thoughts of a warm, sunny, spring day on the Island could not dispel the queasy feeling she'd carried in the pit of her stomach the last two days.

After logging on and waiting a few minutes for the emails to come through, Maggie wondered if she would receive anything other than a few email jokes. The first email that caught her attention was from her sister, Violet. Maggie opened this one first as she knew her sister did not send jokes, but only emailed if she had something important to impart.

The reason for her uneasy feelings became apparent—their cousin Jack had passed away the previous day. Because Maggie had moved away from their hometown in her late teens, she had not maintained a close relationship with Cousin Jack, but she remembered him with fondness. He always had a twinkle in his eye and greeted her warmly whenever their paths crossed. Although a few years older than Maggie, he had been one of the many cousins from her childhood who had gathered at Nana's house as often as their parents would permit.

Nana's warm cozy kitchen was a wonderful place to be as a child. None of the children visiting her house were ever told, "Sit up straight in your chair," or, "Children are to be seen and not heard." She encouraged the youngsters to help themselves to freshly baked big molasses cookies and to sample thick slices of homemade bread covered with stewed rhubarb or molasses.

The sweet memory of Nana holding court in her rocking chair tugged at Maggie's heart. She recalled the many evenings Nana would gather the children around the old cast iron stove. Seated by the roaring wood fire in the rickety ladder back chairs or snuggled up in a blanket on the hardwood floor, they delighted in hearing her ghost stories.

Within the telling of a few stories they would huddle closer together in case an otherworldly spirit reached out and touched one of them. Why even a playful knock on the wall or door would send them into fits of screams! The screaming would be followed by gales of nervous laughter once they realized it was a prank.

Nana was Maggie's grandmother and a great-aunt to Jack. Most of the stories Nana told were of seeing ghosts of the departed and other happenings of the paranormal. Nana had either experienced these supernatural encounters herself or heard the stories from her grandparents when she was a child.

Some of Nana's stories were of seeing spirit orbs. She said the round balls of light were vehicles used by angels to watch over us. Another one of her stories was about a tall, unknown man, always carrying a lit lantern, dressed in top hat and his good church clothes, and seen walking into the graveyard every evening.

BANSHEE WOMAN

Along with the never ending visions of departed souls still seen by the living, Maggie's favourites were the stories of the wailing fairy lady known as the Banshee.

Stories of the Banshee were commonplace in Ireland and Scotland at the time of Nana's childhood. Nana seemed to have a personal relationship with the Banshee; she spoke of the Fairy Lady as a beloved member of the family. Nana had maintained that the Banshee, if one had been assigned to your family by the ancient Goddess, could follow descendants of the Irish and Scottish clans—even when they settled in other countries.

Maggie thought of her family's Banshee, and wondered if she had been at her home on Prince Edward Island and made those mournful sounds on the night Jack died. Maggie had suddenly awaked from a sound sleep around 3:00 A.M. to what she thought was the wind or an animal howling right beside her bed. She remembered three long soft *woo* sounds that were loud enough to get her attention. G.W., Maggie's husband, was lying beside her and his even breathing indicated he was in a deep sleep.

The next morning she had asked him if he had heard any coyotes or foxes howling close to the house. G.W. replied that he had not heard anything during the night and, although a light dusting of snow had fallen, there was no evidence of any animal's tracks around the house.

He added, "This year I have not seen any coyotes and I think a lot of them have been killed off for the bounty that is imposed on them." G.W. then proceeded to tell her about a recent coyote contest on the Island. A cash prize was given to whoever brought in the biggest coyote and that would certainly have reduced their population.

With the knowledge there wasn't a coyote or fox nearby; Maggie, now, after hearing that Jack had died, felt the long repetitive *woo* sound she heard was the death message delivered to her by the Banshee Fairy lady.

Maggie remembers Nana saying, "The sweet, sad death wail of the Banshee is also an indication she is mourning the loss of another member of the clan's transition from the earthly realm."

Maggie emails Violet back and asks if she had any premonitions, such as the Banshee warning, of the passing of their cousin Jack. Violet is fifteen years younger than Maggie and she has not been exposed to the stories of the spirit world from Maggie's childhood.

Because happenings of the supernatural or paranormal were talked about as a natural phenomenon in her formative years, they are now just part of everyday life for Maggie. Nana passed away before Violet was of an age to understand the stories.

Nana had been a devoutly religious woman and faithfully attended her church on a regular basis. She did not feel knowledge of the unseen spirit world made anyone any less of a Christian.

Anxious to hear more about the Banshee and the death warnings, Violet forgoes using email and phones her sister.

Maggie takes a long sip of her now cold coffee and then vigorously scratches her head with both hands as she wonders how she is going to explain to Violet about the ancestral female spirit known in Irish mythology as the Banshee.

Maggie explains how traditionally a woman, known as a *keener*, would sing a lament at a funeral. Keening not only meant singing a lament but howling out in grief as well. Sometimes there were more than one keener at a funeral and the women who were best at keening were in great demand in those times. The more important a person in the society or clan, the more keeners were present at his funeral.

To have a supernatural being such as a Banshee keen at your death was a great honour to the Ancients. It meant you were a person of great integrity and widely respected in your community. If a respected High King was to die, besides human mourners, there would sometimes be more than one Banshee keening at his death. It was the highest accolade to have the powerful combination of seen and unseen forces mourning the world's loss of a great person.

According to legend, the Banshee was connected to the Celtic Goddess of War and Sovereignty. She could appear as a triple goddess: a beautiful young maiden, a stately matron, or as an old woman. When the Banshee wailed the death lament she seemed to appear as an old woman with long flowing hair and light coloured flimsy garments. Sometimes she wore a hooded garment of a light transparent colour.

Nana had explained the Banshee as being similar in some ways to the winged Greek messenger-god Mercury, because, in those olden times, with many wars, there was no human way of communicating quickly. The Celtic Goddess of the earth, the protector of the King and his people, with her great powers of magic and divination would appear in one of her three disguises, the Banshee Fairy Woman, at the home of the deceased to warn the family. The Banshee's mournful wail would be heard by the family at the time of death, and the family would know a loved one had just fallen in battle.

It was usually a week or more after the Banshee's warning before the family received the official word of the father or son being killed.

Some have described the death message as a wailing sound totally penetrating through the family home. Others have thought the mourning sound originated from the sky and it could be heard as if the Banshee was circling the outside of the house. Others have met the Banshee lady face to face and were terrified by her wild look; long tousled hair, whitish gray transparent appearance and the bloodcurdling shrieking. It should be remembered she is also mourning for the family member who has passed on. Some descendents of the old clans only hear a sweet, sad mourning wail or the sound of a harp as she sings the death lament.

Maggie wonders how many descendants of the old bloodlines could still hear the Banshee's death message. It has been said she also can be heard by musicians and poets. Even in our hectic modern world, Maggie is sure, if one listened carefully, her message can still be heard today, but it may come through a different media.

Nana had told stories of how the Banshee was able to change her form and shape-shift into her beloved animals of the earth. Maggie knows of times when, in order to deliver the death message, the Banshee appeared as an owl and, also, as a raven. Another time, instead of sounding the death cry, she simply opened the locked door of the home where the family of the deceased lived. But these are stories for another time....

Tom Rath

Originally from Southwestern Ontario, Tom first moved to the Island in 1979, and lived in Charlottetown for two years before being posted abroad.

Following postings in England and Chicago, and several years in Ottawa, Tom took early retirement and moved once again to the Island.

During a ten-year period as Innkeeper of Lady Catherine's Bed and Breakfast, he welcomed thousands of overnight guests to his adopted P.E. I.

Tom is an active participant in an eclectic mix of trade and community organizations, and has been named the Eastern Princc Edward Island Chamber of Commerce's Member of the Year, and the Tourism Industry Association of Prince Edward Island's Operator of the Year. He has published *Lady Catherine's Kitchen, You're An Islander,* and *The KittenCat Adventures*. He just released a new expanded edition as *KittenCat Adventures: for a Special Person* with more poems particularly for young cat lovers.

He now resides in Upton, about twenty minutes from Montague, with his wife Fran and their cats, Black and Watson. He enjoys creative and non-fiction writing, and his works appear in several Island publications. Other interests include photography and cooking.

Bargain!

Few words stir the heart like that familiar cry, "Bargain!" We'll buy something we didn't even know we needed, if the price is right. That's why, each late September, many of us will hit the roads of Southern Kings again, as eager and excited as any tourist from away. The lure? Seventy miles of garage sales, yard sales, barn sales and stop-by-the-roadside sales.

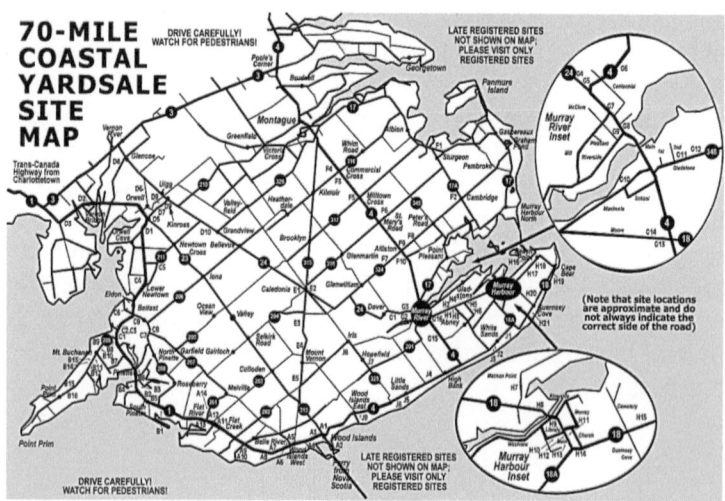

Tom Rath: Bargain!

The beauty of a yard sale is that every single item on offer is something once purchased (or made) by somebody just like us. There are kitchen items, records and books, once-stylish clothing, furniture, knickknacks, and occasionally, true treasures of a bygone era. Some items still work. Some never did and never will. But that's okay, too, if only to justify that impossibly low offer you're going to make.

If you've never heard of the *70-mile Yard Sale,* you must be new 'round these parts. This is an annual event so popular that highways, byways and country lanes from Wood Islands to miles outward are filled with traffic on that weekend.

So empty the trunk and fill your pockets with bargaining power, then head out for the sale. Don't worry about dinner. You can eat and drink to your stomach's content, thanks to the many food and drink booths that will line the routes. But don't waste too much time stopping for a snack. Not when there's 70 miles of bargains waiting to jump into your car!

Island Foods—
It Doesn't Get Any Better Than This

From dawn to dusk, visitors and residents alike can sample a variety of tastes, all fine products of Prince Edward Island. Whether you patronize one of Kings County's many restaurants and dining rooms or pick up your own at the supermarket, Island foods just can't be beat.

For breakfast, try some fresh-sliced Kings County strawberries spooned over Island blueberry pancakes or waffles. Need a little topping? Real whipped cream from Island cows will fit the bill perfectly. One robust eye-opener enjoyed across the Island is the coffee roasted right here on Prince Edward Island.

Come dinner time, a roll filled with tasty chunks of PEI lobster goes down just fine—particularly with a glass of Rossignol wine or a Seaman's soft drink.

Mid-afternoon on a hot summer's day, a cone of your favourite Island ice cream is a welcome respite. Just warn your guests not to order anything larger than a small one—after all, it's equivalent to a double-scooper in many places!

PEI lobster appears again at suppertime, as the classic entree served in the shell. Starters include Cultured Blue Mussels, steamed in wine with chopped carrots, celery and onion. Some folks prefer pan-fried Sea Scallops served over salad. Many consider Malpeque Oysters the best anywhere. The traditional side dish is PEI potato, either as a salad, or baked in its skin. Veggies come from the Island too, ranging from broccoli and cauliflower to fresh red tomatoes and zucchini.

Finally, in the cool of the evening, a dish of Island raspberries is so refreshing. To satisfy that sweet tooth, you can add a little wedge of potato fudge to the side of the plate. Then it's time for bed, to dream of more Island treats tomorrow.

Harness Racing

It's another sunny summer day. Island breezes whisper their cool, refreshing sighs, but wait…there is something else being carried on this gentle wind—a distant rumbling, a male voice squawking from some far-off loudspeaker, and the roar of voices, young and old, rising in a crescendo of excitement at one the most popular sporting events on the Island.

Pulling into the large parking lot at *Red Shores Driving Park Entertainment Centre*, you are struck by all the changes on the site. As you had read in the Guardian, what was once the tired old *CDP* back in 2005 has since been transformed into a sparkling new facility—home to major music concerts, a gambling facility, and quality dining options.

You're here, though, for the horse races—perhaps for the first time in years.

You step from the car, and see people standing tightly against the rail, feeling the thunder of hoofs pounding against gravel and the breeze of buggies passing by. It's already race two, but then there many more to come during this summer afternoon. You head inside the new building to pick up your program and perhaps grab a bite of lunch in *Fractions Lounge*. As you place your order for chicken wings and salad, your eyes take in the room—comfortable tables and counters, television monitors, huge windows looking out to the track, encircling the original wooden tower used by announcers.

While you're waiting for your food, you make a quick tour of the building. Across the hall, through a curving entrance, you hear and see the hundreds of slot machines with their teasing promise of instant riches. Back in the two-story-high foyer, photos of jockeys, races, and other historical mementoes fill an entire wall—each photo visible at close range as you climb the stairs toward the *Top of the Park* dining room. Through glass doors, you peer in at people enjoying fine dining and a glass of wine, eyes flickering between tableside monitors and the track far below the large windows.

Then, it's a quick dash downstairs to pick up your own food order, and look through the afternoon Race Program.

Harness racing has been popular on Prince Edward Island for over 125 years, and has become more accessible than ever for both regulars and newcomers.

The busiest period at the new *Charlottetown Driving Park Entertainment Centre* is *Old Home Week* in mid-August. Islanders and tourists by the thousands come to the annual Fair to enjoy the food, craft commercial and agricultural exhibits. They try a few rides and games of chance along the midway, and make their way to the track, where they can urge on their favourite horses in a daily lead-up to the prestigious *Gold Cup and Saucer Race*. This year's purse is estimated at $60,000.

As you read through the program, you see that today is one of 80 race dates at the driving park this year, and that the monitors above your head show simulcast races from other tracks as far away as Toronto and New Jersey on a year-round basis.

Unlike many other spectator sports, you are invited to bet on the results of individual races, selecting your favourite horse(s), and wagering on which ones will finish in the top three positions. For true aficionados, this selection process entails extensive analysis of a particular horse's track record and physical condition, the jockey's ability, current weather conditions, and a multitude of other technical factors. If you're like most betters, however, it's more a matter of using gut-feel to pick a winner.

You make your choice for the fourth race, place your bet over at one of the busy wickets, then work your way through salad and wings, watching the race and listening to the crowd outside.

Horses round the final turn on the half-mile track, spurred on by their drivers, the enthusiastic crowd, and their own will to win. You find yourself standing and holding your breath, then cheering as you realize that clutched within your greasy fingers is a winning ticket.

Whatever your selection method was, you know that cashing in that treasured souvenir is a sure-fire incentive to planning your next "day at the races."

Lighthouses—Beckoning Beacons

Sailors depended upon them to help ensure safe passage. Now tourists and residents alike recognize them as an interesting attraction. Of 16 un-manned full scale lighthouses on the Island, seven of the more intriguing are located on the Eastern portion.

Point Prim

Take Point Prim, for example. The Island's oldest, this brick tower (now covered with boards and shingles) has operated since 1846 at the end of a long peninsula south-east of Charlottetown. It was automated in 1969, and still assists traffic entering Hillsborough Bay, Northumberland Strait and Charlottetown Harbour.

Wood Islands

Further east is Wood Islands, just next to the ferry from Nova Scotia. Built in 1876, it is now home to numerous activities sponsored by the Wood Islands Development Corporation.

Cape Bear

Further east again is Cape Bear, now moved to the site of the Marconi Station credited with being the first Canadian location to receive and forward distress signals from the sinking Titanic.

Panmure Island

Looking down at beaches on either side of the causeway is Panmure Island lighthouse, located on the southwest extremity of Cardigan Bay.

At Souris East, a sixty foot tower has operated since 1880.

Tom Rath: Lighthouses—Beckoning Beacons

East Point

From there, a short drive takes you to East Point, one of the most popular and busiest on the Island, helping navigation of both deep sea traffic and inshore/offshore fishery operations.

St. Peter's Main was established in 1881 and can be seen by visitors en route to the Greenwich peninsula.

PEI Maple Syrup

Warm days, cool nights, and a dedicated neighbour's toil mean that many Islanders each year will enjoy fresh Prince Edward Island maple syrup on their fruit waffles, pancakes, and other breakfast dishes. I thought you'd like to see a bit of how this incredible taste is brought to life.

It starts off, as you may recall from school day learning, with holes punched into maple trees. In the old days, a *spile* would allow sap to drip into a metal bucket, as demonstrated here by Max Newby of Woodville Mills, near Cardigan.

Nowadays, the syrup travels from the tree by tubing, to a shack where it drips into a specially-constructed apparatus where magic takes place. By gathering sap from trees across his property, Max is able to produce as much as 80 Imperial gallons of syrup a year, depending upon the weather, the sweetness of the sap, and other such factors. Did you know, by the way, that you can also make Birch Syrup? It takes a lot more sap, and it's a much different taste experience.

Tom Rath: PEI Maple Syrup

Max keeps a hot wood fire going, and the liquid gradually condenses from 40 gallons of sap to just ONE gallon of sweet syrup! The result? A natural product that some cooks use not just on certain breakfast items, but also to marinate Salmon Filet for gourmet evening meals. It's also a tasty souvenir for visitors to take home.

Of course, processes are much more hygienic these days. While 35 years ago, you might have found someone sampling sap right out of the tree, nowadays what you're more likely to find is Max's wife Mary Cameron completing the final steps to produce a pure and tasty supply of P.E.I. sap, ready for the table.

The Best Souvenir

Have you ever wondered what visitors to Eastern Prince Edward Island take home as a souvenir? I'll bet you can name a few right off the top of your head.

Let's start with food and beverage. They can find tins of hot-pack lobster and lobster paste, PEI potato chips, wines from John Rossignol, and a fine assortment of Island sweet and savory preserves from practically every community. We have a goodly share of quality artists and artisans working their magic in everything from oil and watercolour paints to pottery and ceramics, knitted and crocheted items, handsome quilts, and baskets. Because our end of the Island abounds with talented musicians, there are lots of CDs and tapes for guests to take back with them.

Visitors can attend classes and learn how to make their own souvenirs in felt, caning, painting and other arts/crafts. Many visitors will go home with a suitcase full of photos and videos to show to their neighbours and family members. Some will even strap an old lobster trap to the roof of the van, and carry it hundreds of miles back home.

But here's the most important fact: The word *souvenir* comes from the French language and means memory. And what every guest who returns will tell you is how treasured their memories are of the time they spent enjoying the friendly people, breathtaking scenery and peaceful feeling of their vacation on Eastern Prince Edward Island.

Shoreline Harvest

That "stuff" underfoot on many an Island beach after a storm is actually an invaluable source of nutrition, beauty products and medical compounds, according to Dr. Irené Novaczek, Marine Botanist. It takes only a few minutes stroll at low tide to gather a bountiful supply of this fascinating plant life from our shorelines.

Seaweed is truly a misnomer. Visitors, and for that matter many Islanders, have no idea of the wealth locked within these colourful aquatic plants. In fact, they are a more concentrated source of helpful nutrients than most land-based plants, she explained, and can contribute to our health in a number of ways.

Irish Moss, the most widely known and plentiful, is a traditional crop harvested by Island families for generations. The carageenan extracted from this plant is typically used as a thickener in food products and as an emollient in beauty and therapeutic products.

Kelp, another seaweed, produces a carbohydrate called algin, which can be used to thicken ice cream, jellies, and even toothpaste. Dulse is dried, packaged and eaten as a healthy snack whose unique flavour and antioxidants are complemented by its provision of B vitamins, iron and fluoride. Skin gels made from these and other seaweeds keep the skin smooth and supple.

Fucus or *wrack*, comes in a number of shapes and colours, and is recognized by the medical community to have significant therapeutic and antiseptic qualities. Brilliant green Sea Lettuce can be used as an poultice wrapped around skin burns and rashes.

Seaweed Pie is just one way to enjoy the culinary benefits of this plentiful natural resource. Dried dulse flakes are an attractive and tasty supplement added to home-baked biscuits. Numerous seaweeds can be dried, shredded and brewed into a healthy hot drink. Seaweed can be chopped and tossed into a stir-fry, and the tender tips of fucus add flavour and texture to salad greens.

Studies underway on the Island and elsewhere have identified seaweed as a commercially-viable means of economic growth for micro-entrepreneurs. Rather than merely shipping bulk supplies to large corporations, family businesses can themselves exploit the inherent qualities of seaweed, and become artisan manufacturers of a range of products created and marketed closer to home.

Tom Schultz

While a professor of Electrical Engineering Technology at Purdue University in Indiana Tom Schultz was drawn, with his wife, to P.E.I. on a vacation about nine years ago. A few years later he retired so they could spend full time at their house in Wood Islands.

He started as a publisher by re-issuing a technical book he wrote while teaching. He subsequently released *Prince Edward Island; Seen 'From Away'*—a book he wrote about his experiences and impressions of P.E.I. He has since published numerous books for local writers including *Still Laughing; Afterthoughts of an Albany Boy* by John Eldon Green, this and the first book from the Montague Writers Guild, and six other books written individually by authors contributing to this book. He has an ongoing project to write a book about sailing.

In addition to writing and publishing, he is active in photography, teaching a course on the subject at the Murray Harbour Community School and producing photo-products supplied to gift shops. Additional activities include sailing, Bible teaching, and forestry. He may be contacted at schultz@pei.sympatico.ca

Driving in the Dark

(Taken from *Prince Edward Island—Seen From Away*)

"The proportion of night hours can either be a burden or a delight." The number of daylight hours in the winter is quite small compared to most of the US (but nothing like northern Canada!). The latitude of PEI compares to Northern Michigan. We find nighttime winter driving intimidating. With so little traffic, there are seldom any lights to mark the road's direction—there are few approaching cars, hardly any house lights, and almost never a car ahead going the same way. The road is often wet and sand-covered so I cannot see the centre yellow line and hardly any road has a white outer line to guide on if a car does approach. Add to that the narrowness and lack of a clear sense of where the shoulder begins and it is easy to see why most drivers hug the middle unless forced to move over by on-coming cars—and even then some folks seem to take their half of the highway out of the middle!

The ultimate challenge is to drive in heavy snowfall at night. Not only can you not see the lines; if the snow has built up you may

Tom Schultz: Driving in the Dark

have no clue where exactly the road is. Many roads have soft shoulders and then a very wide grassy verge that the ploughs use to hold the snow piles. With their outer wing-ploughs, a truck can create a very smooth surface that looks like the shoulder but is actually a smooth pass by the outer plough that conceals a 30 cm. drop. My wife vividly recalls easing over on the imaginary shoulder one winter and getting so stuck she had to get Loren Panting to pull her out.

On a more positive note, one of the highlights of the winter has been driving along the Shore Road (the southernmost road going from Wood Islands to Murray Harbour) for a community school night class. That stretch has one long view of Northumberland Strait and Nova Scotia on the far shore. When the moon is out and the Strait has filled with ice, the view can be spectacular—the water is bright white and the near shore is dotted with dark spruce clumps. Across the water, I can see all the yellow lights of civilization sparkling and, depending on the cloud level, sometimes lighting up the sky. I get a little shiver of excitement—I'm travelling along almost alone with the lights of the houses along the road casting a different mood over the stretch. I can imagine I am someone stuck out in the cold, shut out from warmth and light, looking longingly in at happy families and warm houses. It is easy to look in. More than half the houses leave shades up and curtains open, so you can see in in detail—even to the point of seeing what TV program they are watching. This on-view lifestyle is a rural thing—unlike densely populated areas, there are few bad people outside, so there is no need to shut out the outside world for security at night. It may be the same reason many folks here do not lock their houses or even their cars.

More Prince Edward Island Tales

Incredible Supplemental Health Care

In considering the pieces to include in its collections, the Writers Guild discussed whether "dark" pieces ought to go into what is intended to be a positive but truthful view of PEI. In the end, the only group requirement was that any piece ought to reflect life on the Island. As you have seen from other pieces, history, nostalgia, and daily living have prominent roles. It is in the last category that I present this essay.

A few years back Pixar/Disney released an animated film called, *The Incredibles*. It had lots of action for kids, but there were also sub-plots of interest to more mature viewers. While Mr Incredible is whiling away his time as an inconspicuous, retired superhero, he is stuck in a job as a claims representative for a big insurance company. There he sits, stuffed in his tiny cubicle, with the job of rejecting legitimate claims of poor, elderly widows who have submitted requests under their insurance policies.

That resonates strongly with my experiences with a Supplemental Healthcare insurance company, Atlantic Blue Cross.[1] We have now three times incurred bills for care while in the US. The first time my wife got something in her eye and could not get it out with eyewash. Somewhere in Pennsylvania, with great difficulty we tracked down a low-cost public clinic. We carefully followed the pre-approval steps but, in the end, the claim was denied—the caregiver was only a nurse-practitioner, and not covered (apparently if we had gone to a full-fledged emergency room the several hundred additional dollars would have been covered!).

The second time, an *urgent care* clinic visit while seeing the grandchildren in Indiana was made due to a cold/flu that hung on for

---

1. Incidentally, for those of you not from Canada, while *Universal Health Insurance* coverage pays most everything when a resident of the particular province is sick enough to be hospitalized, *supplemental* coverage is vital to fill in holes in the basic coverage related to prescription drugs, emergency medical care while on trips, ambulance rides, and optical and dental needs. Please note that while I name my particular insurance company, I have no reason to believe other suppliers are more compassionate or responsive—I suspect it is a result of cost containment gone off the deep end.

several weeks. The visit was again dutifully pre-cleared with the Blue Cross 800 number. Arriving home, we submitted the paperwork and waited. The prescription reimbursement arrived promptly, but coverage of the clinic visit was denied for lack of the proper paperwork—no *diagnosis* code. Atlantic Blue Cross requested the additional data but the US clinic apparently forwarded it to its usual US Blue Cross contact which failed to communicate with the Atlantic Canada one. By the time we noticed it, the 6-month limit for the PEI provincial insurance claim was about to expire. Somehow, with lots of noise on my part, the $100 was reimbursed to us.

Oddly enough, I was told by Blue Cross that the requirement for *originals* of documents reflected the PEI requirement, not their own requirement. Face-to-face-contact with the actual person (a sympathetic bureaucrat in an office in Montague, PEI) revealed that *he* is quite satisfied with *copies*. Reporting this to the Blue Cross agent elicited a vague response that that was news to her and was unlike requirements of any of the other provinces they deal with!

Forewarned is forearmed, so for the third instance, arising out of a later grandchildren-visit, when my wife came down with what seemed to be strep throat, we again pre-cleared with Blue Cross, but also made very sure we got an *original* of the doctor's form. The $10 for the penicillin-type medication was paid promptly and the rest (~$130) was denied! Why? The documentation, which carefully had a diagnosis code, failed to include a *treatment* code on an official, universally-accepted form?! Blue Cross did not dispute that she saw a real doctor, but the lack of an official, original copy of an international form. (Why would a penicillin prescription not convince anyone that the doctor was treating strep throat?) In my mind I saw Mr. Incredible in his cubicle. We are still pursuing this claim and monthly calls have tracked and encouraged communication to the point where the paperwork is finally on someone's desk in Moncton (but she was very busy and hadn't gotten to it, we were told—again the separate-cubicle syndrome).[2]

---

2. Notes: as of the revision in mid-May, we had just received the urgent care reimbursement! As of the final revision in early June, we got the glucometer reimbursement.

Fine, you say, but those are all out-of-province issues. Consider a fourth claim: I was recently diagnosed with diabetes and needed a glucometer see how well I can manage my blood sugar. Conversation with the local pharmacist revealed that, to get the meter and test strips reimbursed (at 70%), Blue Cross requires a doctor's prescription submitted with the first-time bill. I called Blue Cross for confirmation and was told just the same thing. Purchasing the glucometer and strips out of pocket (~$70), I carefully mailed in the originals of the paperwork. *Boom!* Back comes another rejection—I had submitted no official *diagnosis,* as well as the wrong payment receipt! (Now I ask you, why would a doctor prescribe a glucometer if there was not a diagnosis of diabetes?) Since we were leaving the next morning (to visit the grandchildren of course), I sent the insurance rejection and receipts to my doctor's office with a plea for help—I hope someone in his office can generate whatever Blue Cross decides it must have. Can you understand why I would pray for good health when visiting the grandchildren?!

So, if you should come to live in Canada and have dealings with Supplemental Health coverage, be kind to the person on the other end and visualise poor Mr Incredible—the representative of a host of poor folks trapped in a bureaucratic Hell, like him forced to earn their living refusing payment. Such a picture helps me to be more tolerant—I realise there are more victims than just the clients.

Wood Heat

(From *Prince Edward Island: Seen "From Away"*)

"Heating with wood is one of the most effective ways I know of to economize." Oil prices keep rising while incomes do not. Particularly in rural areas of the island, wood is often the primary heat source. We have a 1½-story house of the four-room-down-two-up size that we've remodelled into an open plan that heats nicely with a single, centrally-located wood stove. Convection takes care of heat distribution and the catalytic converter makes the stove quite sparing of wood—especially since we have blown 6 inches of cellulose insulation into the walls and added perhaps 12" in the attic.

Every year we have enough wood just from trees that die by themselves or are blown over. It takes less than three *full* cords (4' x 4' x 8') to heat our house for a winter. We use the fact that all the wood we need costs nothing to justify keeping the house much warmer than we would if we were heating with oil, spending thousands of dollars a year for it and depleting the world's limited reserves. Using our own fallen trees as fuel, if we do not burn them for heat they will eventually rot in the woods and our forest floor is already rich from fallen trees of the previous centuries.

Unfortunately, virtually all the trees on our property are softwood. They burn just fine, but spruce and fir need a restricted air supply if they are not to burn up too fast in a glorious hot burst. Larch/tamarack wood (here called "juniper") burns well, but birch and cherry are better. The prime overnight wood for us is maple because it is heaviest and provides heat for a longer time. A neighbour prefers to burn beech—even better, I'm told—but we have none, and it will be 40-70 years before even our maple and ash seedlings mature! Purchased firewood here is inexpensive by city standards—especially if you get several cords of logs delivered at once. We recently got four cords of 8' maple logs delivered in one dump from Ryan Wood Producers for $100 per cord. Such logs are a by-product of the softwood harvesting. While it takes some work to cut these logs to stove length (called *chunking*), most of the delivered wood is small enough in diameter to need no splitting.

Wood heat is not for busy families on the go. In the old days mom or grandparents were always home to add a few logs over the day and it fell to the children to bring in wood for the day. As retirees, wood heat works. You may have heard the expression, "Keep the home fires burning." Decades ago we tried wood heat and gave it up because of just that challenge: we would get up to a cold house, build up the fire, leave the now warm house to go to work, come home to a cold house, build up the fire, and go to bed in an again warm house—an endless cycle of building up fires in a cold house and not benefiting from the warmth—all the work and none of the benefits! At least in the rural parts of the island, with few winter jobs, there is usually someone there to tend the fire. Many folks occupy their winter days cutting and splitting wood. Saving perhaps $3000 in oil costs by making use of otherwise idle time is probably a better deal than working if you include travel expenses and income taxes.

Sailing to Victoria

I really want to take my sailboat *somewhere*—anywhere. Most sails have been short, out-and-back, several-hour trips from the home mooring at Wood Islands.

I select Charlottetown as the destination. In perfect conditions it is about a half-day sailing trip and, if the wind cooperates at all, less than a full day. To avoid time pressure, I block out four days (three overnights) for the trip—two days each way. Several intermediate stopping points are along the way. My wife, Jill, withdrew from sailing for several years—some bad early experiences—but she agrees to give it a try when I plead, "I cannot imagine enduring several days of close-quarters living with anyone else." A route following the shoreline gives her the security calling friends by cell phone and being rescued within the hour!

After enduring all my chatter about boat improvements, she gets to field-test the interior. Is the kitchen (*galley*) suitable for cooking and washing up? Is there enough storage space and counter area? Are the sink and toilet (*head*) adequately arranged for clearance and storage? Are the sleeping accommodations comfortable? If my modifications were well conceived, a four-day trip should prove it.

Wednesday. Jill has highly-refined skills for preparing lists and packing supplies (from our trips to visit grandchildren). She stows everything in boxes or big bags for loading on the boat. While such a short trip could use fresh food, we decide to try out a canned menu. The ice chest is cooled with two home-frozen 4-liter jugs of water which, as it thaws, can supplement the drinking water. Coming in late summer, we disagree on sheets and blankets or a sleeping bag.

For loading supplies, I have brought the boat over to the wharf—rowing supplies from shore to a moored boat in a dinghy would entail several trips with a high risk of dropping something overboard. We park and unload the car just beside/above the boat. I balance everything on the timbers that edge the wharf while Jill drives the car back to the parking area. The tide is so low and the wharf (on the ferry side) is so high, I must stretch up to reach the boxes as she hands them to me. I just set them on the deck for now.

More Prince Edward Island Tales

In true mariner tradition, I avoid the use of the outboard motor and sail out of the harbour. I raise the sails *first* and *then* cast off—if some part of the sail setting causes a holdup, I can give it full attention—no drifting around worrying about running into land or another boat. With the sails set and the boat tugging to start, Jill casts off the last line holding the boat to the wharf while I steer away from the dock. The wind is behind us and we pick up speed.

One of my better decisions is to give Jill *carte blanche* in arranging things inside. As we get under way, she is inside investigating the storage areas and busily stowing supplies. Soon we are through the steels and turning west.

The first leg of the trip takes us west along the southern coast of Prince Edward Island. With a moderate wind out of the north, we make good time. A boat can use the wind to sail any direction except straight into it (up to about 45 degrees on either side). Heading west, a north wind comes from our side—an excellent situation (called a *beam reach*) which can move a boat faster than a wind coming directly from behind. It is a beautiful day—we could not have asked for a better one to begin the trip. With the short distance we are travelling, we keep just far enough off shore to miss any shallows, and navigation by sight is adequate. Since we've driven along this shore many times, it is fun to try to pick out landmarks from our new offshore perspective.

With ideal conditions, I persuade Jill to take the tiller. Quite quickly she is again handling the tiller like a pro. Managing the helm takes practice to avoid over-steering—it is tempting to make frequent corrections, but it is better to hold steady long enough to see if a slight shift in direction is going to cancel out as you cross over to the other side of the wave. With Jill is established at the tiller, I am free to adjust sails and generally look around.

Somewhere along that first leg we hand off and Jill fixes lunch—perhaps canned Ravioli and tea. Our tiny butane stove can go low enough to avoid the blow-torch effect. It even includes an igniter, so turning the control all the way on gets the flame started.

After heating food, the single burner is put to work heating water. Washing up—my job, since the house rule is that *the one who cooks does not do the washing*—is quite easy since, for any meal, dishes consist of a pan, two bowls, perhaps a plate or two, and a few pieces of silverware. The sink is quite shallow, so the pot serves as the dishpan.

I pre-rinse the dishes in the salt water tap to get the food off and then pour a little now-boiling water into the dishpan, add enough cold water to make the soapy wash water endurable to the hands, and wash the handfull of dishes. Rinse water comes from excess boiled water or from the fresh-water tap. A small dish-drainer which fits beside the sink, so the clean dishes air-dry.

Within three hours Point Prim appears on our right. We round the point (far enough out to miss the shallow water where the point extends out to the west) and head northwest across the bay. It is reassuring to have a depth sounder!

The direction to Charlottetown harbour mouth is off the wind just enough to still allow the north wind to drive us. Never having gone this way before, it is difficult to pick out the exact destination by sight and we have to go by compass direction taken from the chart. As we get closer, we make out the Blockhouse Point Lighthouse.

Up until now there has been very little boat traffic—perhaps two fishing boats and a sailboat all day. The closer we get, the more boats we see— apparently in the afternoons many boaters from Charlottetown go a short way out into the bay and then turn back. As we reach the channel that leads from Hillsborough Bay into the inner harbour, the heavy traffic—predominantly motor cruisers—becomes annoying.[3]

Despite the wind coming from the north—just the *wrong*

---

3. If you wonder about how boats pass each other, the general rule is the same as for cars on a highway—you stay to the right side (*starboard*). Unfortunately a good number of these powerboats seem oblivious to another rule that gives the right of way to a sailboat, and I have to take action several times to avoid powerboats (and even a sailboat under power) which are heading in. The exception to the rule is big ships that cannot manoeuvre quickly or draw too much water to leave the channel, but all the problems we have are with small, highly manoeuvrable cruisers whose operators apparently believe they are on a highway and all cross-traffic must yield— no matter what!

direction for going in through the channel—I zig-zag (*tack*) back and forth to tryk to make the entire trip without the motor. The channel is at least 1000 yards wide, so we can travel some distance on each tack, gaining us *some* distance toward our destination. As an hour slips by it becomes apparent the falling tide is emptying the harbour, and we are gaining nothing—the current is dragging us out to sea! Finally I admit defeat and start the motor. In short order we are at our anchorage near the marinas where all those power boats had gone hours ago. My stubbornness cost us time, but we still arrive with plenty of light.

When scouting the area weeks before, I had settled on an anchorage to the southwest of the Charlottetown Yacht Club. Other boats regularly anchor there, and there is a spot on shore where the dinghy can be left with other small boats. I had even checked at the yacht club to make sure I was not going to irritate someone unknowingly. The general attitude seemed to be that I could do whatever I wanted as long as I didn't need dock space. The charge for an overnight berth (if any are available—not likely at this time of year) would be $43, and, by the way, the charge for use of a shower if not paying for a berth is $20!

Enjoying the long daylight of summer, Jill starts heating supper in the now-stationary galley. The wind is light and the water is almost flat. Dinner is served in the cabin at the collapsible table. Then we change the setup for sleeping. My wife soon finds her outer bunk too claustrophobic, so I set up one of the inner bunks. Eventually we settle on bringing one of the outer bunk mattresses down to the center as her bed and I take the opposite outside bunk.

About then I look out and see a sailboat going by to the west with a spinnaker set. (A *spinnaker* is a large balloon-shaped sail used when sailing before a light wind.) Soon there are multiple boats going by with spinnakers. There must be 15 boats silently going back and forth. They sail to the western edge of the several-mile-long harbour, turn, pull down the spinnaker, and sail back to the east. At that end they turn, raise the spinnaker, and repeat the process.

I later learn Charlottetown boasts a sailing club and that Wednesdays are *Spinnaker Night* (Mondays are the ordinary racing nights). I have never thought of boat *racing* in terms of sounds, but on that relatively quiet evening there is no sound to notice. What a contrast with the noise of an auto race! At dusk a raucous horn sounds from the mouth of the yacht club entrance and the boats all disappear.

Thursday. The next morning the decks are all damp with dew and yesterday's clothes are clammy. Dressing and stepping out on deck, I discover a moderate wind out of the northeast, so I propose to my spouse (a lump of covers in the middle of the cabin) a before-breakfast start to use the wind while it lasts and avoid more motoring.

"Fine."

I wouldn't choose to start so early, but there is the lure of the favourable wind. The sun is already up and the sky promises a quickly-warming, clear day. A boat one can get under way without rousting everyone. Breakfast can wait and nothing has to be packed before starting out—just raise the sails, pull up the anchor, and off we go. I am still perfecting the technique of sailing directly from an anchorage while avoiding neighbouring boats, but after mentally changing tack and route several times as the boat swings at anchor, I get underway without hitting surrounding boats. The wind allows us to sail directly out of the harbour without further tacking. As we pass the mouth of the outer harbour, the water is nearly calm. The wind that started us out at a good clip, slows, but comes back somewhat diminished once we get past the shelter of the forested shore.

Breakfast, when Jill fully surfaces from sleep, finds us in the outer bay. It is bread & butter and hardboiled eggs. I have to stay at the tiller, but we eat at our leisure since we will be sailing for many hours. Again, Jill stows everything. She seems happy to have charge of such things—perhaps it gives her a feeling of control—or maybe she just wants to be able to find things again!

The first day we made such good time we decide to continue on west instead of going home. We head off southwest to pass south of St. Peter's Island. The chart shows the ship channel heading straight south before opening up at a buoy, but since we draw only 3', I decide to cut off the corner and sail directly toward the southern coast of the island. The same chart shows that some of that area gets very shallow at low tide, but we are nearer high tide—no problem. Then the depth sounder begins to report 6', then 5', then 4'! With such a broad shallow area which way do we turn to get back to deeper water? We veer more to the south and still see shallow water. Fortunately the depth transducer is mounted 18" below the water line, so we actually have an extra margin, but it cannot report depths less than 3'—a report of 3' could mean 4 ½' or anything less.

We can look down and see a bit of the sandy bottom, but the water is not very clear. Praise the Lord, we eventually start to see the depth increase again—6',
7', 8', 9'. As we come around St. Peter's Island the depth holds just fine and that worry is past.

Apparently the island is a bird refuge, but we only see large numbers of Cormorants. These birds float with just a head and neck sticking out. They are deadly fishermen, "flying" under water to catch fish. They seem interested in us, gathering just in front and then flying off in bursts, only to land 50 yards ahead. Finally we leave them and we continue on west toward Victoria.

As we travel, the wind shifts more out of the east. Jill is by now a skilled helmsperson, so I go forward and get out the spinnaker—the only sail that does not reside on deck. While ordinary sailboats have to have a *spinnaker pole* in order to keep the base of the sail spread out, because our trimaran is so wide the spinnaker can be set from the two outer hulls. It is a challenge to raise a spinnaker because the light nylon material seems to enjoy twisting. When it is finally up we are going faster—3 knots instead of 1½. It certainly does makes the boat look colourful.

Sometime in there we have lunch. We watch the shore but now we are beyond our usual driving region and can't identify landmarks. The chart shows Victoria to be the first place with any sort of shelter for boats, although, if the waves die down we could anchor near shore in any inlet that is deep enough. But how to get an accurate overnight weather forecast?

At our slow speed we seem to make little progress. Looking ahead to the west, several times we think we see the village before the real Victoria appears. I tell Jill to steer directly for the wharf while I lower the spinnaker. Suddenly she lets out a shriek—the depth is rapidly decreasing! Looking at the chart, I see there is a narrow dredged channel from the south. We turn left and *motor* (I have learned something!) between the red and green channel buoys to the wharf. There seem to be no places where we can safely anchor, so we pay the $20 fee and tie up along the wharf. Since the tide ranges about 6', I make sure to run long lines and put out lots of fenders.

Folks are walking out to the restaurant at the wharf end or just enjoying the quiet evening. It is unsettling to have so many people stroll by and look down on us—Victoria is a summer tourist destination with a playhouse and many shops. We feel like animals at the zoo, grateful for the curtains. After supper we take a walk too. We remember several used book shops from previous (by car) visits and find several are still in business and open in the evening. Returning to the boat, we settle into bed and, by sunset, find things have quieted nicely .

[*This is taken from my coming book,* Never the Same Mistake Twice, *which should be published in 2011. It will recount the rest of the trip as well as covering other sailing trips and many technical issues of boat modifications.*]

Kim Smith

Kim and her husband arrived in PEI in May 2008. They'd packed all their belongings in their semi, tossed in their three unsuspecting cats, and experienced an incredible journey driving from Vancouver Island to Prince Edward Island, over-nighting in truck stops all the way.

Kim wrote as a teenager, then stopped, and thought she'd never write again. However, the move to PEI has opened the floodgates of her creativity, and despite her penchant for procrastination, she has managed to amass a fair number of stories and essays in the past two years.

She's had several articles on writing published in an online women's site, two articles published in *Countryside Magazine,* and placed 2nd and 4th respectively in PEI and Nova Scotia literary competitions.

Other pursuits include reading, baking, collecting chicken eggs, and keeping her husband fed as he works on the house. You can read her blog at www.peihome.wordpress.com

Prince Edward Island is Not Vancouver Island
(and that's just fine by me)

"You've taken me to the moon," I said the first time I saw the red beaches of Prince Edward Island. Not only are the beaches a surreal shade of brick-red, the island soil is red, as well. The earth I till for my garden is red and the unpaved roads are red, but the dirt stains on my white clothes are most definitely not, rather they've washed out into a pleasing shade of pink. The white hens are also stained pink, courtesy of the rooster's amorous attentions. I'm sure if I let my white cat outside, she'd be sporting pink paws at the very least.

While the soil on Prince Edward Island is a startling color, it also possesses an uncanny knack of morphing into glorious red mud at the first spit of rain. As I clomp around the property, my gumboots feel like concrete as two pounds of mud adhere to each sole. No matter how much I bang those boots against the sill, the mud tenaciously clings, reluctant, it seems, to be cast aside. The only way I eradicate the mud is by spraying each boot with the hose, an effective way of cleaning the soles, but also a sure-fire way of soaking my jeans.

Before my husband and I moved to PEI, we'd heard vague, unsubstantiated rumors about the presence of mosquitoes. However, without knowing anyone who lived there, it was difficult to confirm. Perhaps I should have randomly phoned some of the residents and conducted a survey. In our first PEI June, we had our answer.

"I don't know if I can live here," my husband moaned.

"I know, I know," I said. "This is unbelievable!"

Unfortunately, mosquito season had only just begun. We tried to go for walks, only to be chased home by ravening hordes. I emerged only to feed the chickens, or to feed hubby, who was in the process of constructing our house. There was no escape for him. We smothered him with *DEET*, but he was none too pleased with its smell and toxicity—tried the mosquito-netted hat, but he couldn't see. Finally, we paid big money for a mosquito-killing machine, and if not for that, I'd be typing this from BC (just kidding). Our second summer, the skeeters didn't seem as bad, probably a result of our fatalistic acceptance combined with hearty denial.

But let's not forget the black flies that leave permanent scars on my body, and the horse flies that circle endlessly around my head, and the tiny little gnat things that land on my skin in swarms and drive me berserk. I also have to mention the June bugs that attacked our windows one night by the hundreds, until the frenetic clacking of their heavy bodies hitting the glass spurred us to switch the lights off and go to bed early. The next day, their dead bodies littered the patio, and for days I winced as I crunched yet another one under my shoe.

I did know that PEI was said to be windy, but I had to live here to truly appreciate that fact. Winds regularly reach 50 km/hr and higher. I recall our first big storm, which blew in at 90 km/hr. The previous night I'd spoken with a farmer regarding a straw delivery, and I'd mentioned the anticipated high winds.

"How high?" he asked.

"Ninety kilometers!" I said.

"Ah, that's nothing," he responded. "You should have been here for Hurricane Juan back in 2003."

"Hurricane?" I shrieked. "They get hurricanes here?"

As for that first storm, I thought our travel trailer (where we were temporarily residing) was going to blow over. The shingles blew off the chicken coop; anything that wasn't nailed down ended up in the next field or wasn't found at all; and all the bird-feeders blew out of the trees. My big fat geese, that couldn't fly if a fox was chasing them, caught updrafts that sent them soaring as though they were eagles. The chickens smart (and scared) like me, hid inside.

As for winter, well, I'm sure there's nothing I can say that hasn't already been said. For a woman from the 'banana belt' of Vancouver Island, the first winter was a wake-up call. Vancouver Island does get some cold temperatures, maybe down to -10C, but the thing is, those temperatures don't last. Within a day or two, the temperature will return to its usual above-zero position, and often stay there for the duration.

But here, boy, it just gets colder and colder, and let's not forget the wind! When it reached -25C (wind chill -35C) our first winter, I thought I might faint with the horror. Feeding and watering the chickens ceased to be fun at this point: my nostrils actually froze together! I was not amused.

Snow is also a rare occurrence on Vancouver Island. Also, it doesn't drift. Snowdrifts took on a whole new meaning here in PEI. I screamed when I opened the door one morning and faced a six-foot monster reclining comfortably in the doorway. Chalk another one up to experience; at least I had something to write home about.

And the drifts fool you. During one nasty three-day storm we saw the snow-plough lumber up the road. Half an hour later we thought, hey, maybe we should make a run for the store. The road seemed clear so off we went, at a good clip, I might add. Mere hundreds of feet up the road the snow had drifted across the road. We kept on driving, after all, back 'home' if the snow starts at 4 inches deep, it stays at 4 inches deep. Not here! Within seconds our momentum had carried us into such a deep drift that we were high-centered. I marched through the bitter wind and cold and snow to our neighbors who had the good sense to stay inside!

Ah, back to warmer weather. Another PEI phenomenon is the lawn-tractor craze coupled with the incredibly neat, tidy lawns. It seems that every yard, no matter how small the lawn, boasts the ubiquitous lime-green lawn tractor. The grass is mowed to within an inch of its life. I imagine that if one allows the grass to actually grow, the neighbors' scorn would be unbearable.

The plus side of this craze, of course, is that PEI is the tidiest province I've ever seen. I've seen only a few lawns that were messy and unkempt; the rest are manicured and orderly, and pleasing to the eye. My sister recently visited and repeated over and over during our drives, "I can't believe the pride of ownership here. It's like nothing I've ever seen."

Our neighbors were supportive and helpful right from the start, offering their help at every opportunity, and serving us endless cups of tea. Complete strangers arrived on our doorstep, introduced themselves, and all of them said, "If you ever need help, just let us know." I can see lights shining from our distant neighbors, and I take comfort in that, in knowing that I finally have a home in a real community where people actually care about each other. It's a good feeling.

Kim Smith: Prince Edward Island is Not Vancouver Island

And it is so quiet where we live. No traffic noise, no people, and most noticeably, no sirens. All we hear as we sit outside in the summer are birds and frogs and coyotes. Perhaps the neighbor's tractor might be at work, or a rare car might pass by. It is truly peaceful.

So why did we move from BC to PEI, wind, bugs, and winter aside? We lived in the city in BC and we desperately craved the country. We had to fight traffic for twenty minutes to arrive at a single country road that ran maybe five kilometers; we'd slowly drive along and desperately wish we lived somewhere like that. In PEI, it's ALL country, barring the downtown core. As soon as we leave the driveway, we're in the country. The 50-minute drive to town is through the country.

And PEI is incredibly beautiful. As one resident aptly stated, "Every scene could be a postcard." From the green rolling hills, to the patchwork quilt of tended crops and pastures, to the lighthouses and the beaches...to the old London atmosphere of downtown Charlottetown and the grand Victorian manors that line the streets, every aspect of PEI holds its own beauty and charm. We are so grateful to call Prince Edward Island our home.

Things I Never Said Before Moving to PEI

1. *"The strings have POISON on them?"* (This in reference to the farmer informing me AFTER I'd lugged 40 bales of straw off the truck with my bare hands that the baling string had been dipped in rat poison to deter rats)

2. *"Is that snow drift really six-feet tall?"* (Luckily it was only six inches thick)

3. *"SKUNK!"* (we yell this out in unison whenever we see yet another dead skunk as we're driving, so I can switch the air intake to *inside circulation only*—if I'm really quick, the air remains clear of *eau du* skunk.)

4. *"I can't believe I'm picking up slugs with my bare hands."* (To feed the chickens, no less)

5. *"Ooh, this hen is nice and fat. Let's eat her first!"* (And I used to hate the thought of killing anything)

6. *"I wonder if I should sew a little hat for this chicken."* (In reference to a hen with a bald head due to over-amorous rooster)

7. *"I can't see outside!"* (Because the windows are covered by snowdrifts)

8. *"Uh oh, you've caught a skunk. Now, what are you going to do with it?"* (We were hoping to live trap the raccoon that was raiding the bird feeders)

9. *"&*$&#*&*$&%^#%'%%' mosquitoes!"*

10. *"I had at least five people wave to me on my drive to Montague!"* (All strangers, but that's PEI and I love it)

11. *"HAWK!"* (In reference to watching yet another hawk dive-bomb our hysterical chickens)

12. *"I think the side of the trailer just lifted off the ground!"* (The wind was blowing 100 km/hr & we were living in a small travel trailer while we built)

13. *"Honey, the roof just blew off the henhouse!"* (Same storm as #12)

14. *"Don't hug me, Martin, you've got chicken poop on your t-shirt."*

15. *"It's -20C and blowing oh, about 70 km/hr; what do you think the wind chill is, honey?"*

16. *"$*#&%&$##)*$*&% mud!"* (It mystifies me how just a few drops of rain transmogrify nice dry dirt into sole-clutching, soul-sucking mud)

17. *"Does everyone in PEI own a lawn-tractor?"* (Yes, folks, they most certainly do)

18. *"Martin, the geese are eating your insulation again!"*

19. *"Good grief, how many Tim Hortons are there in this town?"* (About 10, I think, for the very small city of Charlottetown)

20. *"Hey, we're the only people here!"* (This on election night—we voted at the Legion just up the road from us)

21. *"What on earth is THAT? Lock the doors!"* (First time I heard a fox yelping outside the trailer)

22. *"This is like some Stephen King novel."* (While listening to hundreds of enormous June bugs slam *en masse* into the windows)

23. *"We haven't seen a car yet, have we?"* (After walking for an hour along our country road)

24. *"Watch out for the snowdrift!"* (Too late, we were stuck one second later)

25. *"Is winter EVER going to end?"*

26. *"Honey, the chicken house just blew over."* (110 km/hr winds—the chickens were NOT impressed!)

27. *"Everybody is just so nice here!"* (In our new community where we've been welcomed with open arms)

Moving Coast to Coast to Live Our Dream

(Published in Countryside magazine Jan./Feb. 2010)

My husband and I recently moved coast to coast, from British Columbia to Prince Edward Island. Most of our friends and family didn't understand, but for us, the choice was logical.

We both grew up dreaming of living in the country yet both of us have spent all our adult lives living (unhappily) in the city. We weren't getting any younger, and life is far too short to be miserable. We haven't regretted our decision; our lives are so much better than before.

We purchased 25 glorious acres, half in forest, the balance in fields. We do have neighbors but not close to us—there are only a half dozen houses on our road. The silence is blissful. The local wildlife consists of coyotes, foxes, raccoons, skunks and rabbits.

We lived in a travel trailer with our three cats for the first eight months while my husband built the house. In December 2008, we moved into the basement just as the first snowstorm of the year blew in. The basement, with its concrete walls and floors, and unfinished pink-insulated walls, seemed like heaven after many freezing nights in the trailer. We had no stove (and still don't—we are only on 'temporary power' until the drywall is up)—I cooked on our woodstove all winter long, quite the change for a city girl!

It is now July 2009. My husband is currently siding the house—this is a work in progress as we don't have much money and he has to work part-time to keep money coming in. I think it will be a long time before we move upstairs! We recently added a dog to our family.

We have also collected an assorted bunch of chickens, including banties, and are enjoying fresh eggs every day, as well as selling them. In time we'd like to add guinea fowl and turkeys to our farm, as well as sheep and perhaps a Jersey cow. First, though, we have to finish the house and build a barn!

This year is my first attempt at vegetable gardening. I planted a little of everything, and will learn from my mistakes. My husband has killed and processed several chickens, and we hope to raise meat rabbits next year. A neighboring farmer has planted our fields in oats and hay, and this year we will have free oats and straw, and he will use the rest for his dairy farm.

Our neighbors are friendly and always helpful. They often gift us with home baking, and more recently, perennials for our garden. In the winter, a neighbor loaned us his tractor and snow blower; in exchange, my husband would plough his driveway, as well as several others on the street. Any time he needed a helping hand with construction, someone was always pleased to offer their assistance.

A few things I learned along the way:
- Nostrils freeze shut at -25 Celsius.
- There can be a six-foot snowdrift in the doorway, and only two inches on the car.
- Carrying water to the chickens all winter long becomes very tiresome.

Kim Smith: Moving Coast to Coast to Live Our Dream

- Roosters' combs can become frostbitten and fall off.
- Roosters start crowing long before dawn.
- Approximately one million insects and slugs would like to eat my vegetables.
- Squirrels, while adorable, dig up bulbs, shred insulation, and raid the bird-feeders.
- Geese will chew everything in sight, including car trim and electrical wiring.

    I love watching fireflies as they flutter through the trees in the darkness. I love listening to the howls of coyotes on their nightly prowl and to the deafening chorus of frogs in the awakening spring. I enjoy watching the tractors rumble by, and having strangers wave to us as we drive down the road, and seeing the little red flag standing upright on the mailbox announcing, *you've got mail!* I love seeing the great fields of golden wheat and gaudy pumpkins, and beaming sunflowers, and the reds, yellows, and golds of autumn leaves. I love attending county fairs, and driving down lonely country roads, and awakening with the roosters on hot, summer days. It really can't get any better than this.

Every day I wake up and realize anew how blessed we are to be living here. We don't have much money and I know we will face some hard times, but we'll get by somehow. Even if, for some reason, we cannot make it and have to return to the city, at least we lived our dream, if only for a while. I will always treasure these memories as being some of the best of my life.

An Island Evening

Dusk sneaks up and dims my eyes,
Stars emerge and light the skies.
Fireflies flit from tree to tree,
Beacons ablaze for all to see.

Frogs start up in a nearby slough,
A deafening chorus, but impressive, too.
A coyote yips, and more reply,
Ghostly howls drift right on by.

I hear the nearby lighthouse call,
Warning mariners, one and all.
A fox lets loose its eerie moan,
On the prowl for blood and bone.

I shiver 'neath a cooling breeze
Sweeping in from the nearby seas.
It's time for home, and time for light,
Fond farewells to this Island night.

Coyotes

Yips and howls float across the field. Coyotes. I'm still in the open but not for long. "Damn," I say to the dog that stands beside me. All four of our eyes scan the dark line of the trees across the field. Nothing moves. A blue jay swoops over our heads and disappears into the woods, the flash of blue and white swallowed by the shadows.

The dog whines, nudges my leg, and pushes forward through the knee-deep snow. I follow, erasing its paw prints with the rubber tread of my winter boots. "Some shortcut," I mutter to myself. I could turn around, make my way back to Clara's farm, beg a ride home, but I don't.

"Sarah," Dave had said to me this morning as he dropped me off at Clara's. "I don't want you walking home. It's too cold and snow is on the way. You call me, all right?"

"It's a beautiful day. Don't be such a fuss-pot." I smiled at him but he remained stone-faced. "Fine," I said. "I'll call you."

I watched as he wheeled the truck down the driveway, listened for the honk that always came. Just because I was a city girl 'from away' didn't mean I couldn't take care of myself. I'd moved to the Island two years ago to be with Dave, a third-generation dairy farmer, and twenty years older.

I step into the trees, the trail ahead white and unbroken. The dog is running through the brush, searching for hares and squirrels. All I hear is the rhythmic crunch of snow beneath my boots and the occasional excited yip of the dog. No unearthly howls break the wintry air, no piercing shriek of a rabbit run to ground.

Still, I walk faster than usual. It's only a 15-minute walk to home, but the snow is deep and it's getting dark. I should have phoned Dave. Oh God, he's going to be so mad. Why do I do this? He's a good man; I shouldn't push him like I do.

The dog materializes in front of me like a ghost and I utter a small shriek. But it isn't the dog; it's a coyote. Its blood-red tongue hangs between lips lifted in a silent snarl, and I see the gleam of shiny, white canines. Another one slinks from the trees, and we stand frozen in a tableau out of time; the hunters, the hunted, in the infinite seconds before the first leap.

Kim Smith: Coyotes

Something brushes my leg and my heart stops. But it's the dog that rushes by me; it hurls itself at the coyotes with unexpected violence. They turn and run, but not quickly enough; the dog sinks her teeth into a fleeing haunch. The coyote thrashes and snaps and snarls, but the dog hangs on, uttering primal screams as blood splashes scarlet against clean, white snow.

I seize a fallen branch and join the fray, slamming the heavy wood against the coyote's head over and over. The dog finally lets go, and the coyote streaks away into the trees where the other waits, and then they are gone.

I drop the stick and kneel beside the dog. "Good dog. You're a good dog," I sob into its fur. I rub its shoulders and flanks, looking for injuries, but I can't find any. I grab handfuls of snow and scrub the coyote's sticky blood off it muzzle. "Come on. Let's get out of here."

"Sarah!" I leap up. Dave's voice echoes through the trees. The man has come to meet me, thank God for that, and I rush forward through the snow.

"Dave, I'm here!" Around the next bend, and there he is, slogging through the snow with determination. "I'm so glad to see you!" I throw myself at him with a cry.

"Foolish woman," he says. "I knew you'd pull something like this, so I phoned Clara and sure enough, you'd just left." He pulls away, surveys my tear-streaked face. "What happened? Are you okay? I thought I heard the dog barking."

"Everything's fine." I avoid his gaze. "I just was thinking of a sad story from the news, is all. You know how I get."

"Hmm, if you say so." He grabs my shoulders and pushes me ahead of him, towards safety, towards light and home. The dog bounds forward, tail waving like a flag, and I hear Dave's steady steps behind me. I don't look back.

The Farm Wife's Lament

(2nd place in the 2009 PEI literary competition)

If Bessie had one chance to live her life again, she'd do it right. That's what she always told Myrtle, her nearest neighbor, or whoever else stayed long enough to listen. Not many people visited Bessie these days, all of them either long dead or almost dead. *I'll outlive every last one of them*, she regularly thought to herself. *Just my luck.*

"Yes sir," she informed Bob, the mailman. "I'd sure do it different if I had the chance, mark my words. I'd never have married Joe; you couldn't pay me all the money in the world to make that mistake again."

Bob revved the motor of his car. "Gotta go, Bessie," he said. "Lots more mail to deliver." He waved a hand out the window, and quickly pulled away. He watched her small, tidy figure recede in the rear-view mirror and sighed. She had a knack of appearing at the mailbox every day just when he arrived. He'd admitted shamefully to Jack, his good friend, that sometimes he drove on past, even though letters addressed Bessie Jones lay beside him on the seat.

Bessie trudged up the long, narrow driveway, picking her way carefully through ruts of thick red mud. It clung voraciously to her gumboots, and speckled the hem of her navy skirt. Bessie didn't mind. Mud was a fact of life here on the island, and she had all the time in the world to do laundry.

"I'd never marry Joe again," she muttered to herself. "Why would I saddle myself to a man? I could have been a teacher, or a nurse, why, I could have even been a writer!"

The small yellow house waited patiently for Bessie. After her marriage, she'd painted it to match the first spring daffodils, but as the years ticked by, its vibrant color faded to the anemic yellow of a store-bought egg. The porch leaned alarmingly to one side, its wooden floor planks losing their battle with gravity. Joe never had time to replace the single-paned windows, and the walls remained bare of insulation. Bessie declared the house resembled nothing more than an icebox between November and March. Springtime, without fail, the basement flooded, and she washed and dusted to the constant rattle of the ancient sump pump. Come summer, though, the old place was almost tolerable, and it even looked pretty surrounded by the flowers in bloom. Roses, carnations, and sweet peas, pansies and petunias painted in glorious hues of red and pink and white and purple. They colored Bessie's world with a joy that faded with the dying blooms at autumn's arrival.

She'd raised her four sons here, and watched her infant daughter die here, as well. The ambulance took hours to arrive, inching through blowing snow and drifted roads. She understood this, but it hadn't stopped her from raging at the paramedics, and she'd screamed at Joe after they'd left, "I hate you, this is all your fault." He'd stared at her, mute and anguished; he knew he wasn't to blame. Emmy had stopped breathing, just like that, but he never defended himself, and Bessie scorned him the more for it.

But life continued, as it always does. And the desolation that gripped Bessie retreated with the passing years, though she never loved her boys as much after that. As each year slipped away, so did the joy within her, replaced by a mantle of sorrow and regret.

Bessie set a pot of tea to brew, and picked up the phone. "Hello, John? I've just put the tea on, and I've got your favorite cookies in the jar." She sighed into the phone. "I understand, son. Maybe tomorrow?"

"Myrtle? It's Bessie. Come on over for some tea. Oh, you're still not well? Well, get better soon, dear." She set the phone down. *Poor Myrtle*, she thought. *Those treatments are really taking it out of her.*

Bessie took her tea and settled into her favorite chair. She'd nursed all her boys in that chair and crooned them to sleep. Now, she cradled a small white cat that leapt lightly into her lap. It felt solid and warm, its deep throaty purr the only sound in the room. She picked up a notebook that lay on the table beside her.

Why I ever married Joe, I'll never know. Bessie scribbled furiously. Here I am, sitting alone in the living room with only a cat for company. I could be living in a fancy condo in a big city somewhere, with lots of money in the bank and all sorts of friends. I wouldn't have to hang my laundry, or wash dishes by hand. Why, I'd have a maid to do all that, and maybe even a cook!

I wouldn't fall for another farmer. All those years of just getting by, always worried about too much rain, or not enough rain, and whatever Joe harvested, it never quite paid the bills. I hated those phone-calls from the bank, and seeing Joe's sad eyes staring at me over the supper table.

Bessie put the pen down and massaged her swollen fingers. It hurt to write for more than ten minutes. All her bones ached and complained lately, reminding her of her wasted years.

"You know who I should have married?" she'd said to Myrtle only last week. "Young Samson, that's who. If I had to marry anyone, then I'd have picked him. He lived the good life, didn't he? He and Marcia with their fancy cars and houses, traveling all over the place, and lordy, they even sent their girls to that expensive boarding school. My boys sure could have learned something at that school."

Bessie sighed and leaned back. The afternoon sun explored the room with pink-tinged fingers, and cast its gaze into dusty corners. Its warmth settled on Bessie and she closed her eyes. *Ah*, she thought, *now to sleep and to dream.*

She awoke with a start. The doorbell rang loud and harsh in her ears. Cold crept into the room while she slept; the sun had abandoned her until tomorrow. Bessie stumbled into the kitchen, and struggled to open the door.

A white passenger van idled outside. **ADULT DAY-CARE, JUST LIKE HOME, ONLY BETTER!** adorned its sides in one-foot high, black letters. A young woman, *Katie* her nametag read, waited on the porch, one hand steadying an elderly man beside her. He swayed unsteadily, eyes half-closed, as if unaware of the two women.

"We had a great day today, Mrs. Jones," she said. "We walked around the mall and then we had hamburgers."

"Huh, he never cared much for the mall," Bessie said.

His eyes flicked open at her words, and he stood a little straighter. "Bessie." His voice scratched weakly at the cool, still air.

"He never says a word all day or remembers anybody," Katie said. "But when we get him home, he sure remembers you!" She climbed into the van and stuck her head out the window. "See you in a couple days!"

The man shuffled forward, stepping carefully over the sill. He never looked down; his eyes remained fixed on Bessie, who stood waiting.

"C'mon, Joe, I haven't got all day." She closed her fingers lightly around his arm, surprised, as always, at the frailness of bone and flesh. They walked together into the kitchen and Bessie sat him at the table.

"It's leftovers again." She pulled a plastic-wrapped plate from the fridge and placed it in the microwave. The scent of roast beef and potatoes soon drifted across the room. Joe shifted eagerly in the chair, face alight with anticipation.

The microwave beeped five times. Bessie pulled the plate out and peeled back the plastic wrap, releasing fragrant clouds of steam. "I made oatmeal cookies today," she said. "You can have some after supper with your tea." She set the plate in front of him, but he pushed it away with sudden violence.

"Bessie," he said. "I hear Emma crying. Can you hear her?"

"Hush, Joe, it's only the wind." Bessie leaned over him, tucked a lace-edged napkin neatly around his neck.

"You better go, Bessie, she needs you." He was becoming agitated. The wooden chair legs creaked alarmingly as he rocked back and forth.

"She's okay, Joe, Emma's okay. I took care of her. It's just the wind you're hearing." She lowered a hesitant hand upon his head and stroked him, soothing him as she would one of her children. He stilled under her touch, and moaned softly with pleasure. Her hand stilled on his soft, fine hair.

Joe smiled up at her. "You're so beautiful, Bessie," he said. "I'm the luckiest man in the world." He reached up to touch her hand, but it was already gone.

"Hush now, Joe," she said. "Your supper's getting cold."

My Life in P.E.I. an Update

As I write this, it is May 8, 2010, the two-year anniversary of our arrival in Prince Edward Island.

What an amazing adventure this has been, and we're still on it! I managed to survive the second winter in PEI, although I must confess it was a gentle one according to all the locals. Even I realized this when the dreaded blizzards never materialized, and the temperatures plummeted to -20 for only a brief time. The snow had all melted by late February, and the robins were singing 'spring is here' from the treetops.

We are still in the process of building our house. My husband has done most of the work himself, as well as working four days a week, so it won't be finished for a while yet.

But that's fine by me. Spring is here and I'll be outside anyway. I'm contemplating my garden—it's a mess, I must confess, compared to my neighbors' gardens that are already tilled and partially planted. Gardening really is a lot of work, no I take that back: *weeding* is really a lot of work!

We've accumulated a veritable farm—two calves, one goat, and two sheep, too many chickens, one goose, two ducks, and three pigeons. We also have a dog, and we still have our three cats. We've even joined the PEI Purebred Poultry Fanciers' Association, and have won ribbons with some of our chickens!

The last two years have been good to us, and I'm looking forward to many more here in beautiful Prince Edward Island.

Linda Stewart

My name is Linda Stewart (nee McCosham), daughter of Leonard and Marjorie; wife of Brian; mother of Matthew; grandmother of Claire, Jesse, Meadow, Julian, Mathias, Faith, Theresa and Isobel; sister of Mark, Leo, Cathy, Rudy, and Shannon. I live in Wood Islands. I am also a writer and fiddle player (sometimes fiddling teacher) and, since 1981, a Christian who is trying to do it (Life) right, but as the song goes, "God's still workin' on me...."  The main themes of my poetry are faith, nature—especially the island beaches—snapshots of everyday domestic and family experiences, music, and lots of other stuff.

I will never forget the thrill of seeing my first published piece, *Simple Country Pleasures*, which appeared in the October 1990 issue of *Common Ground* magazine. When I took a risk by sending in the hand-written copy—I did not even own a typewriter, yet—it opened the floodgates of my creative writing. My poetry, essays, and short stories have been published in literary journals, anthologies, and magazines throughout Canada, the U. S. and in many fine P.E.I. publications. My chapbooks of poetry include *The Piper & The Poet, Isle of My Heart, Water & Spirit,* and *Mornings & Haiku.* In the photo, I am signing a copy of *Water & Spirit* at my book launch at *The Reading Well* bookstore in Charlottetown.

I am a six-year cancer survivor and, a couple of weeks prior to the writing of this bio, was kicked out of the cancer treatment centre for being too healthy.... My most noticeable, lasting side-effect from the experience: curls!

I am a member of The Montague Writers Guild, a former member of TwiG, a member of The Queen's County Fiddlers, and The Southern Kings Fiddlers. I attend Central Christian Church and teach violin/fiddle at The Centre for Performing Arts.

While I have been, for the most part, a stay-at-home mom, I have ventured, at times, into the outside world of work, but home is where my heart is. The sight of a stack of Chocolate Brownies under the glass dome of a cake stand gives me a satisfying sense of accomplishment...and then I'll sit down and write about it!

Cow's Milk

Just over the hill from our place lived a neighbour with cows. My father often helped out the older farmer and his housekeeper by giving them drives into town or to the grocery store. In return, the farmer gave us fresh cow's milk, as opposed to goat's milk, or store-bought milk. Each day, I was sent over with a pail which was promptly filled with milk. I would often bring one of my friends with me.

The first trip over, the kindly housekeeper gave us a cookie. This was an added perk we enjoyed very much. So, on our next visit, we looked forward to more than the cool, bubbly milk. We sat expectantly on their kitchen couch, our legs dangling out in front of us, not yet long enough to touch the floor. The lady of the house fetched our milk and gave it to us. We thanked her, then waited. Since we did not immediately get up to leave, she made small talk and was very polite to us. As the conversation waned, we sat silently, still waiting. Finally, the housekeeper told us sweetly that we could go, now. Disappointed, I said, "But aren't you going to give us any cookies?" She chuckled and asked, "Oh, is that what you've been waiting for?"

She went to the pantry for the cookie can. Still smiling with amusement, she warmly said, "Certainly you may have a cookie." We reached our small hands in and took one each, said "Thank you" and took our leave. But we were slightly embarrassed as we walked and nibbled our way home.

Simple Country Pleasures

I am back to my serene country home after a shopping trip to the city. I have my *Beethoven Violin Concerto No. 1* playing on the stereo and a pot of *Peaches & Spice* herb tea on the stove. I am using my beautiful blue and flowered tea cup that I bought at an antique store in Wellesley, Massachusetts. There is no noisy traffic outside but lots of birds singing and bees humming. It will soon be time for the pleasant task of purchasing a new journal. This quiet country atmosphere is very favourable for writing. Thoughts and ideas are able to flow freely and to a writer the keeping of a journal becomes not only a pleasant luxury but a need. For I believe that a true writer will always write whether it is the writing of novels, short stories, articles, or simply keeping a diary. It is as necessary as our daily bread. These simple pleasures do much to impart peace to home and hearth, quietness to the mind, and health to the soul. No fast-paced living for me, thank you. The quiet country life is just my cup of tea.

Rich in Simplicity

I've always had green fields to roam,
sunshine and wind
to play 'round my face and hair.
The Father sends me gifts
of sparkling crystal waves,
music of the finest note
from heady poplars rushed
by summer breezes,
and gardens of imaginings
to turn ordinary days
into empyrean soirees.
I've always had these,
always had love,
always been rich
in the beauty of simplicity.

My First Visit to Woolworth's

I have never forgotten my first visit to Woolworth's in Charlottetown when I was four years old. It was a frightening experience as I became separated from my mother with her in one aisle and myself alone in another. My bawling drew the attention of other shoppers. A young couple came to ask me what was wrong. I looked up into their kind, concerned faces and kept bawling. Does a four year old get embarrassed? You bet. I was as humiliated by my wailing as I was scared to be all alone in a big store full of strangers. It seemed like an eternity, but my mother quickly found me. There she was, pushing her way through the small crowd that was beginning to gather around me. How glad I was to see her. My little four year old world was right again.

Looking for Partridge

A sliver of moon and a star punctuate the twilight. Old apple trees, aged spruce, and birch trees, are sepia forms, their branches gnarled against a pearlescent sky. Mere moments before darkness falls, it is time to look for the Partridge silhouetted in those crooked limbs. While the evening meal is simmering on the stove, I peer out the window to search for their dark stout bellies perched amid the leafless tangle. This is now my habit, learned from older family members who appreciated the nature found in their own backyards.

Sweet Offerings

Ribbons of notes drift lazily
through afternoons of sunshine
and swaying spruce.

I picture rolling hills
and salty seascapes
while the fiddler plays
his peaceful tunes.

Little boys jump through sprinklers;
a grandfather watches and smiles
from his shaded bench.

Here, at Eden,
the silver maple leaves dance
to the fiddler's bittersweet strands.

Life could be one continuous
slow-air melody;
poet's dreams need never stop.

Island flavours would always be
salt-wind and rosebreath,
never-changing in simplicity
and stillness.

The fiddler's sweet offerings
pour over the soul of the day,
enchanting its most common hours.

Marjorie's Place

(for Diane & Madeleine)

Our family and their's
were intertwined
for the past fifty years, plus.
I remember visits there
as a little girl.
Nothing about the house
ever changed.

My aunt and her friend
from Ontario and I
made it our mission
during their summer trip
to the island
to visit the old McGuigan place.

No one was home
but we wanted to see the renovations underway
by the new owners from British Columbia.

We peeked in the windows
to see fancy new cupboards
and a modern open concept
in place of the little pantry,
where Marjorie would disappear
to bring out cookies and a pot of tea.

The new wrap-around veranda
held a handmade wooden swing.
We took turns sitting in it and having our photo taken.
We giggled and had fun
in our boldness and, later,
had to endure scoldings from others
when we giddily confessed to our trespassing.

Linda Stewart: Marjorie's Place

*I loved sitting there
on that swing
on that veranda,
enveloped in the intoxicating peace
of the soft July breeze
through trees....*

*Iona...
My father
grew up there,
just across the road
and up a bit.*

It could be home...

My Island

*The mystical magical
shades of life
escape not my attention
in these island shores
where the cliffs are red,
the gulls loud, and the sea
a salty rolling blue.
I am alone on this island,
it belongs only to me
because this island lives in my heart
in a place no other soul
has been able to reach.
The loneliness of the island
is a friend
understanding me too well
and the winds that sashay
across its wide open expanses
seduces me into fancying
that herein lies eternity
where changes never occur
and where time does not exist.
I want my island
to stay the island of long ago
where old buckets hang
from farmhouse gates
and wagons sit isolated
in fields of golden hay
and dusty clay roads wind
through hills and valleys
in silence and solitude.
This is my island,
my mystical magical eternal island.*

Kitchen Sounds

*They must love
these kitchen sounds:*

*the clink & clatter of dishes;
the oven door closing;
a pie, casserole,
or a roast sliding
across the rack;
the oven door closing
quickly shut again
with a sharp squeak.*

*They know that supper
will soon be ready,
something comforting and tasty.
The anticipation is delicious.*

*My husband and our son,
who now towers over him,
wait like happy
well-cared-for children.*

*Sometimes I think
that I would like to be
the one listening
to kitchen sounds.*

Native Islander

*I do not step
ever-so-gingerly
over the stones
at the beach,
on my way to the shallows
and sandbars,
like some pussy-foot tourist
or city dweller.*

*I trod like the native islander
that I am
over the mass
of stone, rocks, shells, pebbles...
my bare feet accustomed
to such prickly, piercing, pressing terrain.*

*I want the visitors
on the beach
to know at a glance
that I am not one of them...
I belong to this "cradle in the waves"
born and raised here.*

Ordinary Things on Ordinary Days

Kitty and I are out on the veranda together enjoying the late afternoon summer air and breeze. She is stretched out her full length on the cement floor, eyes closed, while I catch up on some reading. We can hear the traffic down on the highway. The ferry is in dock and another load of passengers and vehicles have been released. A fresh pan of Chocolate Chip Cookies are cooling in the kitchen. I've already taken my walk to the shore and along the beach this morning. The tide was heading out and the beach was washed and tidy. I left my flip-flops up on the bank and let my bare feet cool to the damp, salty sand.

Kitty is stretching even longer and languorously. As long as I am out here, she will stay instead of wandering the countryside. I believe she loves my company as much as I enjoy hers. She will "talk" to me, "Meow, Meow, Meowing" when she is hungry, or wanting more milk, or a door opened for her, or just a little more petting and attention. It is quiet, again, now that the ferry traffic has come and gone. Crows are cawing, the sky has grown overcast. The air is humid even though there is a breeze rustling the branches of the poplars. Perhaps rain is on the way. August is rapidly coming to an end, as I knew it would. I will prefer September this year. The stifling heat was, well...stifling! The way the months fly now, it won't be long until summer is here again! Oh, well, let's not worry about Time. Time is fleeting, but so will those cookies be once I've poured a glass of cold milk! I enjoy reading and writing about ordinary things on ordinary days. With all of the unsteadiness in the world now, the wars, the terrorist plots, I am more and more content with ordinary things on ordinary days.

Coffee

Coffee has certainly evolved. We have been immersed in coffee culture over the past two decades. The nineties gave birth to a coffee renaissance where trendy cafes have popped up around our cities offering the most delectable coffee concoctions—including my favourite Mochachino topped with whipped cream and cocoa sprinkles.

One evening, here at home, I was suddenly struck with a revolutionary idea. To the other three adults in the room I asked, "Hey, anybody want a cup of instant coffee?" Two of them grimaced and said, "No thanks." But my husband, considering for a moment, replied, "Oh, go on, then. I'll try one!" Brave man!

Instead of the usual top-of-the-line brew out of a coffee machine, we were actually going to sip on a cup of instant—*No Name* instant! I keep a jar in the cupboard for emergencies such as running out of the good stuff, or the power going out and being unable to use the coffee machine. I remember when all my mother ever used was instant powdered coffee. There were no fancy coffee percolators in the homes of the neighbourhood where I lived as a child. My mother's coffee tasted delicious—sweet and creamy. I know because I used to beg her to save me the last mouthful. In spite of all the gourmet coffees we have to select from, none will ever taste as wonderful to me as my mother's little cup of instant. I can't seem to make it as good as her perfect cup which is why our forays into the world of instant coffee are few and far between. I might as well tape a sign onto the jar: *For Emergencies Only.*

Morning Walk

This morning I head out for my daily walk earlier than usual. Normally, I walk in the afternoon between 2:00 and 4:00 p.m. Today, however, I am out the door by 9:00 a.m. This February morning is a beauty. The sun shines brightly over the pristine snow and the sky is crystalline blue. I walk snappily down the quiet, tree-lined road, toward the highway, and as far as the old general store (now closed and vacant).

Three or four of the neighbour's cats are playing near the ditch. I say, "Hi Kitties!" They stop and stare at me. I recognize one of them. Our cat brought it home with her on a few summer mornings. It was only a kitten then. I found the two of them curled up together on the wicker chair on the veranda. The kitten, however, was wild and ran away as soon as I opened the door. It appeared thin and I was concerned about the poor thing. I had hoped it would stay and drink a saucer of milk.

Our cat, which I merely named "Kitty" because it was a stray and I am guessing that she was one of the barn cats, wandered into our yard one July afternoon, almost two years ago, meowed back at me whenever I spoke to her, followed me to the clothesline, snuggled into the chair on the veranda, and stayed. Kitty had come in search of a real home, loving companionship, someone to purr to when stroked on the head or tickled under the chin. Kitty wanted a family.

As I walked on, I thought of Kitty wanting out on cold, winter nights, making her way down to the barn, (about a quarter mile), then, purposefully, faithfully, heading back home in the mornings to the wicker chair to wait for me to wake up and let her in. After a breakfast of her favourite tinned cat food, she would curl up on my bed for the day, safe and comfy.

This morning I am relieved to find that the wild kitten not only survived, but appears fully grown and healthy. Besides cats, I notice the fresh-water brook running cool and free and stand for a moment to admire it and listen to its rippling. When electricity fails us, here is a supply of water so clear, so pure, so sweet. My morning walk is not just physical exercise....It is thirty minutes of Zen.

October on the Island

*Autumn leaves strewn across paths,
cool breezes and chimney smoke
curling the night air again
is part of the charm upon -
October on the island.*

*Sweaters are donned, wood is stacked,
pickles stored, and pumpkins picked
for a Thanksgiving Day pie.
The noon sun seems more golden,
the sunsets more orange
in island October skies.*

*Time slows, lamps are lit early,
board games and hot chocolate
appear on hushed, expectant evenings...
all is tranquil, settled
because it is once again—
October on the island.*

Winter Landscape

The seventh snow storm this month is upon us.
Perhaps there will be something lucky in that number seven.
It is a winter wonderland out there.
I stand at the window at dusk to admire the landscape in the soft, pearl light.
The branches of the pine trees are laden with thick puffs of snow. The skinny branches of the rose bushes are fattened with white.
The lane and the lawns are filling up. The sky is one perfect shade of dove gray.
That gray sky is always the sign of snow.
I am inside a house inside a snow globe.
Someone has shaken it and turned us right side up, again, and the snow is falling...falling...falling...

A Boy and His Chickens

(Snapshot 1)

*A boy and his chickens
running through the yard
makes a comical scene.
As the game intensifies,
who is chasing whom?
Round and round they go;
the boys face grinning with glee,
dimples showing,
the hens squawking,
their feathers flying!
Such fun they have!
My boy and his chickens*

Almost Ten
(Snapshot 2)

*Finally, she sees him in the distance
through the windowpane.
Her face beams and she smiles broadly
as she watches him
swinging his plastic bag of goodies
following his first walk to the store alone;
his little face, no doubt, wearing a grin
of triumphant glee
at his new independence and thoughts
of the fun-filled tasty evening
of games and treats ahead,
with friends.*

Profile of an Eleven Year Old
(Snapshot 3)

He likes jelly donuts,
the Chicago bulls,
and drawing cartoons.

He cheats at cards,
likes to hang out
with his dad
doing guy's stuff,

but needs Mom's doting
and good-night kisses.

The gleam in his eyes
spells mischief—
likes to stay behind
during walks
to throw snow balls.

Dimples rival blonde wisps
for adoring school girls'
attentions.

.

Love Notes in the Sand
(Snapshot 4)

*I can hardly fathom, beloved beach,
that you have been here hundreds of years
before I. It seems as though
you have only been mine to roam
and dream upon
but pioneers once walked you
and hauled their boats to anchor
upon your shore. Your red cliffs
are scarcely virgin
spectator to a main of trysts and witness
to a bundle of love notes in the sand:
the purest of which belongs to me:*

I LOVE MOM

102

Leslie Stewart

My name is Leslie Stewart. My wife Dorrie and I live in a big old yellow farmhouse with sunflowers painted on one side of our home, in Sturgeon P.E.I. We used to live in Cambridge, then one day, the Roads Department moved the sign, and now we are fish people living in Sturgeon.

I grew up in Ontario, in the small tourist town of Southampton, on the shore of Lake Huron. My life in Ontario and PEI have similarities. The former had beaches of soft white sand, the mouth of a river flowing into the lake, an island just a mile off shore, and the sun setting into the water horizon every night.

Yet, here on PEI, where some things are the same, others are so different—it is the difference that holds him here, warms him, and brings that smirk to his smile. It is also the adventures and making of friends that will continue to anchor him to the shores of PEI.

I began writing poems in 2007. My first poem was about our neighbour, who would come over and blow out our driveway after a winter storm. I now write about the whole Island, and lands far beyond. I have so far produced three books of my own poetry, *Whats Goin On, Sands of Time* and *Home At Last.* A few poems from those books follow here.

I hope you enjoy what you read. I enjoyed writing them.

Bizarre

Isn't it strange?
Isn't it bizarre?
How we came
To where we are

I was born up
In old Ontario
Came to the island
One I didn't know

Leslie Stewart: Bizarre

In what direction
How could I know?
Some fifty years later
Where I would go

I read some books
The story of Anne
How she was an orphan
Of Prince Edward Island

Little did I know?
But here I am
Living down here
On that island

I'm not an orphan
A small girl like Anne
Heck no! I've come here
As a crabby old man

Father of three
Grandfather of four
And I'm sure soon
There will be more

But as for now
It's ok by me
To be a grandfather
Living by the sea

Isn't it strange?
Isn't it bizarre?
How we came
To where we are

More Prince Edward Island Tales

Grandchildren Come To Stay

When our grandchildren come to stay
No matter the weather, it's a wonderful day
Ours come to see us from far away
When they come by car it takes days

They once flew down for a holiday
Emily and Alice were first to stay
Then Maple brought her parents one day
Yes, these are little girls that come to stay

But in the future a grandson will stay
When we open our door on that special day
Little voices will echo we've come a long way
So grandpa let's go to the ocean and play

We can find snails and shells buried in clay
Grandma and us, found spitting clams one day
And once we used the sand dunes to sleigh
No matter what they say or do in a day

Leslie Stewart: Grandchildren Come To Stay

It's always too short of an island holiday
So sad to see them leave and go away
We know they'll be back another day
Grandchildren are our children in yesterday
It's just we look at them a different way

Their grandfather

More Prince Edward Island Tales

Panmure Island

Down to the sandy beach
To walk the salty shore
I'll take my lovely girl friend
The only girl I adore

I don't need a bottle
Of rum or cheap wine
To keep my spirits up
I have a sweetheart of mine

We stroll on the romantic shore
Catching sparkles in our eyes
Bright loving fireworks
To light up the night skies

The warm island winds
Wash over us, damping our skin
We stroll together as one
Making loving memories within

How fortunate we have become
To find harmony and romance
That bonds my love to hers
I wish others this amazing chance

A stroll on Panmure beach
The sky of brightly lit stars
As the two of us walk together
Forgetting where we are

Memories of Mine

Back long ago, when I was young,
We wandered field and far.
Many island tunes we sung,
With our fiddle and guitar

Our bodies tanned from summer sun
The joy of laughter and tears
When we were young all was fun
On this island we love so dear.

We fiddled and riddled and rhymed
And danced to a grand old time

Watching fishing boats bob in the bay
Reflecting waters of time
Old fishermen tanned as island clay
These are memories of mine

Tunes in our heads, rhythm in our feet
And love in our hearts
That when my love and I did meet
And never will we part.

We still feel the music and riddle and rhyme
Now we sit on old rocking chairs
And watch the young folks dance in time
As joy and laughter fill the air

We fiddled and riddled and rhymed
And danced to a grand old time

Vanessa

*If you have come to the island for a stay
And are looking for some entertainment today
You could check on a Ceilidh or two
There will be one no doubt near you*

*If you're lucky or look real hard
You may find Vanessa Bernard
She can play for you the island violin
Vanessa is tall, attractive and slim*

*Often you can find her singing aloud
With her parents as partners, she is proud
Jackie, her father, leads with his guitar
Vanessa's mother Sheila is never too far*

Leslie Stewart: Vanessa

They say when Vanessa takes to the floor
This step dancer is one girl you should look for
She comes to entertain with fire and zest
As a step dancer Vanessa is one of the best

The audience quiets as she heads to her space
Vanessa wearing a beautiful dress takes her place
I feel sorry for the fiddler's fingers right now
As soon as the bow crosses the strings, its wow!

Vanessa's shoes are flying, rhythm in her feet
She captivates her audience, it's bitter sweet
Up on her toes, back on her heels and around
I swear sometimes her feet never touch the ground

They say back in Bear River, her hometown
The wooden stage caught fire, almost burned down
Sparks they say flew off her dancing shoes
The metal cleats, had burned right through

Now when Vanessa step dances with such zest
She is entertaining you, doing her very best
At the Sturgeon Ceilidh, we have a water bucket near by
As Vanessa dances faster, those sparks might fly

I've never felt as tired as watching her dance
Just sitting in my chair, my heart starts to prance
It's the greatest workout I've never done
Watching Vanessa dance, she's a marvellous one

You can see the pain on the fiddler's face
Vanessa has danced to a furious pace
She sees he is hurting, his fingers are sore
Vanessa slows down, then dances no more

We all take a well-deserved breath for working so hard
Believe me, it's hard work watching Vanessa Bernard
So as I was saying before all this began
You should try to see Vanessa if you can

Day Dreaming

I was dreaming of a better time
Oh, a different life you see.
If I could only find that damned genie
Three wishes she could give to me.

I would wish of traveling, maybe in the sun
Get that golden tan; go on the beach for a run.
Instead back to the clothes line, another sheet to hang
The sink is full of dishes, now the telephone rang.

Can somebody answer that call, I'm busy
Father sleeping on the couch, oh is he?
The vacuum quit working, the washer on the blink
And now I see more beer bottles, covering the sink.

I would wish for the finest clothes fit for a queen
Jewels of diamonds, gold, emeralds so green
It's the ball diamond and rings around the collar
Hey Julie, it's supper time, give your brother a holler.

Their clothes are too small or just worn out
Wake up your father give him a shout.
Dinner is made, now food is on their plate
In twenty seconds their food they will have ate.

I would wish the man I married, ten years or so ago,
Still looked handsome, tall and thin you know.
I must be doing the washing wrong, the ironing at that
I see his shirts have shrunk; his pants are short and fat.

Yes my life has become quite busy, raising all these kids
I've had the nine children, so ask what he did.
He was just a fisherman, spent his lazy time at sea
No wonder folks say, "The children all look like me".

Leslie Stewart: Day Dreaming

Yes, I was dreaming of a better time.
Maybe a different life for me
But this is the only place I would want to be.
My family and the man that fishes from the sea

Look What the Storm Brought In

This island Christmas story is very old
It goes something like this, I was told
A husband and wife aboard an immigrant schooner
Travelling to Montreal, they should have left sooner

The cold north winds and ferocious Atlantic gales
Made traveling across the Atlantic a living hell
Their destination, to Canada, a brighter future it would be
Many times they felt they might just perish out at sea

Their money had run out paying for the passage on this trip
Very little for meals, they often went without on the ship
Others would help them with some left over bread or stew
Without their help in these hard times, what would they do?

The traveling time for this crossing had exceeded by days
Ice had formed in the gulf, causing the schooner to delay
They would have to sail back and try to dock in P.E.I.
The late December storms, large ice fields drifted by

Everyone on board felt the danger, the schooner was in
Approaching Charlottetown harbour, the ice field became thin
Through howling winds and rising sea, they managed to dock
Unfortunately, the ship's hull had been ripped open by rocks

Passengers and crew fought hard to abandon their ship
Salvaging what they could from this nightmare of a trip
In the melee of those running to be saved and those saving
Two people managed to leave, not seeing someone waving

If they had noticed on this stormy Christmas eve
Things would have been different, for the birth of me
With high winds, visibility poor, the couple found their way
Little did they know, I would be born on this Christmas Day

My parents to be, found an empty building, a barn
Inside the protective walls, they came to no harm
They never realized in all their fight to survive
A newborn son, their first, would soon arrive

Leslie Stewart: Look What the Storm Brought In

Huddled in the barn as the blizzard raged outside
The two new immigrants slowly became aware inside
Lots of straw covered the hard clay floor where they sat
The man brushed away the straw with the use of his hat

They would build a small fire, safely for light and some heat
Through the barn windows, faint lights blinked in the street
From time to time, they could hear muffled voices outside
The language was unknown to them, they listened and tried

With the howling winds, most of the words blew away
They would wait for help, in the barn they would stay
Their small fire gave them light, warmth and life
My mother went into labour on Christmas Eve night

Unlike the birth of our baby Jesus in his stable
I had no animals to witness my birth at this stable
Only my mother to encourage me on this day
I was the best Christmas gift, my father did say

It was close to noon, when the storm let us be
It was light shining through the barn window I see
There was some commotion, as some townspeople appeared
From the storm last night, some thought us dead they feared

Someone had smelled the smoke coming from the barn
When the door opened, they saw me in my mother's arms
A baby was born on Christmas Day, in Charlottetown
Three immigrant people hiding in a barn they found

Some of the townspeople gathered, one did say
What a blessed thing to be born, on this special day
We were taken to a house where we stayed awhile
They found us a home, outside of town just a mile

As I was brought into this world on Christmas morn
And my parents brought to P.E.I. by a storm
They would take not another chance with the sea
We stayed on the island, our new home to be

Voices We Hear

Eerie tales of shipwrecks
Those sad souls lost at sea
Lighthouse on Satan's shores
Only a devil's home it be

Ragged rocks beneath the waves
Satan's arm and raunchy fingers
Reach out unseen to you beneath
To tear the hull away if you linger

Stay well away from this place
Take a wide turn or pay the toll
Better to lose a day or two
Then sink and lose your soul

Those voices we hear of souls lost
They're screaming to you stay away
The Satan's fury will draw you close
Hoping to gather more lost souls today

Leslie Stewart: Voices We Hear

Yes it is indeed a beautiful scene
A lighthouse painted all in white
The light shines for your safety
Showing the way in dark of night

But is it the Devil's light we see?
It may be the Devil showing the way
In a storm we can't really tell
Is it the lighthouse saving you today?

The light may be only a reflection
On clouds, angry mist or rolling waves
Check your maps for your location
Or your soul you'll have to save

The screaming you hear in the night
As the waves smash upon the shore
Are the voices of thousands lost
Who sail the wild seas no more.

Listen to what these voices say
Tell the captain of what they said
For if he does not listen to you
Then, very soon all will be dead

Just another shipwreck to talk about
Their sad story of desperate survival
Drowning at sea, no one comes to help
Their families will wait, but no arrivals

Stand on the docks or wait on shore
Waiting for their loved ones to arrive
Instead all the news they will hear
The ship went down, no one survived

All were lost; no one was found
The worst storm in centuries
Friends and families, ship and crew
All perished in Satan's seas

Sands of Time

While sitting on a driftwood log
Gazing sleepily out towards sea
Digging in the sand with my toes
As the children in my memories

Oh, how long has it been?
A small boy digging in the sand
Using our mothers kitchen spoons
Making sand castles when we can

My sister and I, digging in the sand
Playing on the beach, running around
Digging for that gold buried beneath
But, all that gold we never found

These are memories of mine
Of a time long gone by
Playing in and on the sand
A tear now slips from my eye

Leslie Stewart: Sands of Time

Picking up a handful of sand
Watch as it runs smoothly away
Just a few small grains of sand
Are stuck to my sweaty hand today

The last small grains holding tight
Much like my childhood memories
How many others have felt this way?
Sitting on a log looking out to sea

How many feet have walked this shore?
How many toes have dug in the sands?
How many people have swum these waters?
How many creatures before the coming of man?

Did Pirates, Vikings, Ancient Seamen
Have they walked this very beach?
Looking and dreaming of their life
And on how old they might reach

The sands of time as we all play
Digging, building, walking upon
As the wind blows small grains away
Our memories live, they are not gone

When you stroll on our native shore
Walking perhaps barefoot in the sand
As you watch small children playing
Or perhaps lovers holding hands

The sands of time are here
Let every living moment be its best
Don't let the winds blow you away
Sit down here on this log and rest

More Prince Edward Island Tales

www.ingramcontent.com/pod-product-compliance
Ingram Content Group UK Ltd.
Pitfield, Milton Keynes, MK11 3LW, UK
UKHW041950230426